A Career in Computer Programming

Stephen Mooney

A Career in Computer Programming

Published by brownmoon designs
ISBN: 978-0-578-91388-9

To my parents Pat and Spike

Who got me started

And to my wife Teri

Who kept me moving

Contents

Introduction

As a child growing up in the 1950's and 60's, we ate dinner every night as a family. During our family dinners my father, who worked for an automobile company as a middle manager, would often gripe about the people problems he had to deal with at work. I grew up knowing I would not like to deal with people problems, or work for a large corporation.

In high school and college I studied chemistry, physics, and math. I found that I enjoyed solving problems. In chemistry and physics this required performing experiments, making measurements, and doing calculations. I was not adept at manipulating beakers, or in taking precise measurements. Later in college I was introduced to computers, and realized that here was a way to investigate and solve a large class of problems that did not require any manual dexterity.

When I entered college, I was interested in learning physics and math, and not particularly concerned about how I would earn a living. When I thought about a career, I wanted to do something I enjoyed. For me this would involve opportunities to continue learning and using the knowledge gained to solve problems. I thought a sufficient income would naturally follow. During my career I slowly realized there was more to earning a living than solving technical problems. I realized that a paycheck ultimately came from other people, and how I related to other people had a large influence on my paycheck.

Over the course of my career I worked as an employee in a small start-up and several other well established small businesses. I worked as a general partner and later as a sole proprietor, in small consulting firms. And finally I worked as an employee in a technically oriented international fortune 500 company.

This is a (mostly) non-technical account of the work I did, as well as my slow education in those non-technical skills needed to earn a living..

Early Interests (1958 .. 1967)

I have always been interested in computation. Not in actually doing the computation, but in the rules for how it was done. I counted on my fingers to add. I barely remembered the multiplication table. I made many mistakes in simple arithmetic that rendered longer calculations inevitably incorrect. I was also very slow to arrive at these wrong results. I never finished a timed math drill in elementary school. I almost flunked fourth grade because I could not do long division. I would write a trial quotient and get a remainder larger than the divisor. I would then try the next larger quotient and get a negative remainder. This was very frustrating. One of my elementary school teachers told my mom that I was not going to amount to much in math.

I was never too concerned, because I was fascinated by the rules for doing arithmetic. To divide by a fraction, you invert and multiply. Adding and subtracting fractions was cool. Later on: The procedure for taking square roots similar to long division was the most clever thing I had seen. How could this work? How did they calculate the value of π? The rules of computation using logarithms were like divine revelations. How were sine, cosine and log tables calculated?

Once I reached the level of algebra, where rules and abstractions were what mattered, I was OK and started doing very well in math class. I eventually earned my Bachelor's degree in Mathematics.

I was also fascinated with calculating machines. My dad brought home a machine that would add, subtract, multiply and divide. I loved to watch the machine divide. It would whirr, roll numbers around, and shift its carriage while doing the problem. The slide rule was also great fun, and I became proficient using it in High School Physics class.

I read several books on computers which explained how they worked. Flip-flops, half adders, registers, core memory, one and twos complement arithmetic. I was disappointed with binary arithmetic. Why couldn't computers use real numbers? It was difficult to turn real numbers into this weird binary form, and when the answers came, they were no good until translated back into real numbers again. I did not have a real serious interest in computers. I was much more interested in Astronomy, Physics, and Math. None of the books I read were about programming. I never made any connection between my love of the rules for computation and what I had learned about computers at this time. Indeed, my high school offered a programming class (in 1966 !) but I felt no urge to take it. I saw a friend's printout from the class. On the page was x = x + 1 and I thought "How stupid. How can x ever be x+1"? I never felt the urge to inquire. I studied Chemistry and Physics in High School, and majored in Physics when I went to college.

Meet the computer (1968)

One day in the middle of my university freshman calculus class, the professor posed the following problem. Solve this equation for X: *Three to the power X is equal to X to the power three.* At first sight it seems there would be no other solution. The professor brought this up out of the blue. It had no connection to any past, current, or future lesson in calculus. He only said there WAS a solution for x not equal to 3. He never mentioned the problem again, or gave the solution. No one in the class asked about it in class.

I became interested in this problem. It seemed like it would be simple to solve. Although I was a Physics major at that time I fancied myself a better than average mathematician. How tough could this be? I set to work algebraically manipulating each side of the equation. It was not long before I came to a dead end. After several days of off and on attempts, I realized that I could not solve this. I had no other tools besides algebraic manipulation.

I now wanted to see the solution, and how it was solved. I would learn something new. Asking the professor never crossed my mind. If I had asked him, I might have started down the path to real mathematical thinking. I lived in a dorm hall with several junior and seniors of mathematical repute. I showed this problem to several of these whizzes. The one with the best reputation also was interested in the problem, and made a serious attempt. After several days he came and confessed he had no solution. He was not interested enough to ask anyone else that he knew. There the problem rested for a few days.

In my circle of friends, there was a guy a year older who was into computers. We were all math and science types. Computers were not yet in common use. This was in the days of mainframes, before microcomputers, PCs etc. The University was experimenting with a new timeshare mainframe. None of this had much impact on us math and science types. Although they were a subject of study, it was not something a serious mathematician or scientist needed to pursue. This guy was a little different because he was knowledgeable about computers, and had access to the timesharing system. Someone suggested I show the problem to Jim. I did. His reaction was totally different than all others. He immediately said "Well let's go find the answer".

It was night, but we immediately walked over to the small building that housed the timeshare mainframe. The place was noisy with air conditioning running in other rooms. The walls were all un-washed white, the floors all dirty white linoleum. The computer itself was in a locked room, and was not visible. The place was very cluttered with large line printer listings stacked everywhere in a dis-organized fashion. In the basement was a room with several teletypes. There were few other people about. Jim sat down at one of the teletypes.

He slowly typed stuff onto the roll of paper and pressed ctrl-xoff to end each line. For each line the teletype made a grinding noise, hesitated for a second, and then rapidly typed a response onto the roll of paper. Jim typed in a simple program in the PIL language. (An early interpreted BASIC-like language). This program just plugged a number in for 'x' into the equation and computed to see if it solved the problem. He started at the number one and added 0.0001 each time. Jim described this as he typed in the program. It took several minutes to type in. Eventually he said "OK, here goes" and pressed ctrl-xoff.

This time the teletype was quiet. For ten seconds. Then it spit out on the roll of paper: X = 2.4781. We ripped the paper out of the teletype and walked back to the dorm. Elapsed time: 30 minutes. Actual computer time used: 10 seconds.

This made a huge impact on me. I got the impression of an incredibly powerful daemon that was serving who knows how many other teletypes, but it never hesitated at all to respond to Jim's typing. Finally we asked it to run this very inefficient, tedious program that ran through a numerical haystack in the most stupid way looking for a needle. In ten seconds it had found the answer.

This experience crystallized all previous tendencies toward computers in my mind. Here was a way to control an awesome power to investigate and solve the types of problems that interested me. It was not yet a career. One could not (yet) major in computers, nor did I want to. I switched to a Math degree, never thinking of making a living in computers. But I took all possible computer classes even though they were for very little credit, and required a ton of work. It was pure joy to go to those classes and listen to the lectures and do the work. Now x=x+1 did not seem stupid at all.

Looking back at this experience, it is obvious that I was never a mathematician. I was interested in algorithmic solutions, not sophisticated mathematical reasoning. Even though I later got my degree in Mathematics, I knew I was never any kind of real mathematician.

Undergrad Computer Programming Classes (1968 .. 1971)

Programming classes were offered as electives. I do not believe that there was an undergrad degree in computers offered at that time (1968). These classes were for minimal credit, and took a lot of time. The lectures were like normal classes, but the work required was coding a bunch of computer programs.

I do not remember much in the way of programming per-se being taught. The first course was FORTRAN 4. The class taught the syntax, and gave a set of programming assignments. The grade depended on getting the assignment to work. If it worked as required, you got an automatic A. If it did not work, then the instructor would look at the listing and give partial credit.

Although there was the beginning of a timeshare system, these undergrad classes did not use it. All the work was done on punch cards submitted in batch runs. The majority of the key punch machines were in the old computer center building along with the teletypes. There were lots of key punch machines, but often not enough, and you needed to wait for one to free up. You would write out the program on paper, then type it onto punch cards at one of these machines. Plop some control cards at the beginning of the deck, and submit it at the batch window.

The operator gave you a receipt card with a number punched on it. A similar card was added to the front of your card deck. You could then look for that number on a batch monitor screen, sort of like an airline flight arrival screen at an airport. If things were running well, your deck was read into the system, processed and returned wrapped up in the output listing within an hour or so. If the computer was 'down', it might take all day. The computer was often 'down' or backed-up from recently being 'down'. So even in the best case, you could get only a few turns a day.

Although turnaround improved at night, I was never there late at night. My inclination was to sleep on it, and try again the next day. Of course, that meant that I could never wait till the last minute to do the work. I came to pride myself on this way of working. With proper planning, I could "Do my business in the daylight". I came to look on all-nighters and late nights as a failure of planning. If lots of work was required, well better get an early start, and keep at it. This attitude was only intensified when later in my career I was locked into a three-hour commute during banker's hours.

Of course at the beginning, the program would not pass the compiler due to various syntax errors and typos. At several hours per run, successful students soon learned to tighten up their typing skills. There were so called "express" key punches where a few cards could be changed or added. This sort of worked OK although some people's idea of "a few" cards was quite large.

The mechanical aspects of this were difficult for me. As described earlier, I did not do well with exacting tedious tasks like typing closely parsed FORTRAN code. But I loved what the computer did, so I knuckled down and put in the effort required to thrive in this environment. I began to notice something. Although the computer was an extremely exacting and un-forgiving judge of my work, once I got the code right it STAYED that way. One could rely on it being RIGHT forever, I could move on and build onto it. I could hold the product of all that effort (the card deck) in my hand, put it on a shelf, combine it with another card deck and it would flawlessly do the desired computation. Once I expended the effort to get it working, I was DONE.

To succeed, I developed a style of bench checking. I would play at being the computer, and "run" the program in my head. Start at the bottom (lowest level primitive) code, imagine inputs, and work through the results. Next start at the beginning of the code, just like the computer, and follow the procedure for different inputs. If you didn't do this sort of checking, you would fail to get the program working due to lack of time. The worst thing that could happen was an infinite loop that used up all of your account's time, and provided zero feedback as to what was wrong. Or spit out reams of paper each page with the letter "W" at the top.

Like any trade, you learned by mistakes. Each mistake was expensive in terms of time and effort, so they were burned into my memory. There were many opportunities to make mistakes, so there was a lot of experience gained. Looking back, I see that I worked in a totally different way then. Back then it was best to create the entire program on paper and check it all out first prior to key punch and trial runs. Because each run took so long, it was not advantageous to create test scaffold code to check out parts of the program separately. The scaffold code itself would be expensive to debug. The idea of creating any part of a program without immediately testing it in some scaffold is anathema to me now. This is one of the biggest changes in the trade of programming during my career.

I can also see that some of the practices that worked well then still work well now. Since there was zero support (for students) for debug at the time (Other than a complete core dump), I got into the practice of printing out information about progress and intermediate results. In this way I avoided a run where I got back one page of totally blank paper with no idea of what the program had done. Although I later used symbolic debuggers with breakpoints a lot, I have always been most comfortable with the technique of displaying progress as the program runs. Thirty years later, while programming embedded systems with no debugger available, these instincts and techniques were still current. I got all of my programs to work. As I recall it was a process of self-teaching, since the class work was un-related to any of the finer aspects of programming.

Another programming class I took as an undergrad was actually a grad level course in assembly language. This was the IBM 360 assembly language. The work was still card deck based, but the projects were more advanced. There were text parsing and numeric conversion projects. Assembly language allowed for a new debug tool: The core dump. I soon learned to treasure a good dump. I learned to keep looking at the dump even after I found the immediate cause of failure. Look at stuff that seemed to be working OK. Often I could see other errors that had not yet manifested themselves.

Although it is true that once you gain experience programming in one language, other languages are easily learned, this only goes so far. You can easily use the new language in the same manner you used for the old language. This can be effective and productive, but it is not really learning the new language. That still takes doing work and making mistakes in the new language. It seems that I needed to switch languages on an average of every five years. Each one had its quirks, strengths, and weaknesses. I never did this unless forced by my job. I always started resenting the loss in productivity, and ended up becoming an expert in the new language.

One of the most rewarding programming classes I took at this time was on numerical methods. How to find roots for equations, solve systems of linear equations. This addressed my interests in computation directly. One of the best results of this class was my relationship with floating point numbers. The class dealt primarily with floating point numbers and their foibles.

My mathematics courses had pounded into my head an abstract way of thinking about numbers and computation. But this course emphasized the very specific behavior of floating point numbers in a computer. It finally hit me that computers did not manipulate numbers at all. Floating point numbers in a computer, indeed integers in a computer were not numbers at all. The names just mislead the unwary. The computer was just manipulating bit patterns. These bit patterns could be associated with mathematical numbers under certain circumstances. It was fascinating to learn what those circumstances were. Binary numbers, decimal numbers, ones complement, twos complement, packed, unpacked: it was all just various ways to manipulate bits as a tool to solve problems.

All of the mathematical expression syntax in languages like FORTRAN or 'C' are just cute syntactic sugar. You must never look at "numerical" expressions in a computer program as mathematical statements. The rules the computer used for different kinds of bit manipulation were easy to learn, so it was no big problem to think this way. But thinking this way really speeded up debugging.

First Job (1969)

In my junior year (1969 - 1970) I was asked if I wanted a part time job helping out on a programming project. I think my good grade in the assembly language class put me on someone's list. I did not know these people. I said "sure" and so started my programming career. This was part time during the school year, but full time the next summer.

Some academic project had just gotten (or would soon get) a new PDP-11. They needed a cross-assembler that would run on the IBM mainframe timeshare system. An assembler is a program that translates machine code from a human readable form to the binary form that the machine hardware understands. The native PDP-11 assembler was considered a total joke. Besides, the timeshare system offered file sharing and archival etc. The cross assembler was to be implemented in IBM 360 assembly language, and the PDP-11 assembly language it would parse was invented by the project to look very similar to IBM assembly language. There was no thought at all for PDP-11 conventions and compatibility. It was only years later that I even thought to question this decision.

The cross assembler was designed, and was in the process of being implemented. I think it was more work than the designer bargained for, and was much less glamorous than the main work of the project. (Early, pre-TCP/IP computer networking). I was hired to take a large role in implementing the assembler. I started with the task of implementing symbol table processing.

This was my first large assembly language project. The external interface was designed. There were many runtime constraints, but no internal design. The symbol table had to have fast performance with possibly a very large number of entries. There was no support framework. Just the OS and bare IBM 360. For the first time I came close to failing. Because of lack of experience, it was difficult to keep all constraints and the complex internal structure I came up with straight in my mind. On this project we typed our code into files on the timeshare system. No punch cards. I still needed to write it all out on legal pads first and simulate it at my desk first. This project approached the limits for which this technique would work.

I don't remember much about the design I came up with, except that I faced failure, and trashed my entire approach. I started over with a simpler internal design and got the job done. Of course, I could have never come up with the simpler design without first agonizing over the failed design. It was a harrowing experience, but I learned the limits of brute force, and the power of a higher level point of view when designing complex sub-systems.

Later, I heard talk about "top down", versus "bottom up" design methodology. Generally, "bottom up" was sneered at, and "top down" was accounted the best. I found myself unable to pick just one. I would always start out at the bottom, and try and design low level constructs that would match the external environment while simplifying the problem. Then I would switch to top level design that used these new low level constructs. This would point out where the low level constructs needed to be changed in order to make the high level design "elegant", or "robust", or "simple". With this high level context in mind, I would re-think the low level constructs and how they related to the problem. This could iterate a few times, especially since new information about the problem to be solved would be trickling in all the time.

If I tried to stick with a pure "top down" approach, I would often find that the low level interfaces did not suit the external environment. Then there was a strong temptation to make these low level interfaces complex, or keep complex state information in the lower levels. After all, with a computer anything is possible. Moving back and forth between high and low level designs allowed me to put the complexity in the least complex place.

I stopped feeling guilty about my inability to do proper "top down" design when I started reading about the history of Mathematics. There I found out that, contrary to the top down way Math is taught, it was all invented bottoms up.

The summer of 1970 I faced a dilemma. Go back to the automobile plant and make $3.95 an hour (with opportunity for time and a half for overtime), or continue working on the programming project at $3.00 an hour. It was a dilemma because my parents were paying for that part of my college bills that I could not pay myself. Any less money I made would need to be made up by them. I chose to continue programming.

Endian Issues

Another of my assignments was to implement the assembler's so-called data section. These assembly directives were used by the programmer to initialize portions of the program's memory image with arbitrary data. I was looking at the PDP-11 book and trying to fit the data formats into the IBM type assembly language syntax. I saw something that made no sense.

I re-read the description of data layout many times. The integers seemed to be placed in memory with the least significant byte first. Was this possible? Was I miss-reading the book? This way of storing data in memory was backwards. What about text strings? Was each pair of even / odd characters swapped or not?

I went to the professor in charge of the project. He briefly looked at the manual, and said "No, there is no problem here". He explained that the IBM manuals numbered the bits in diagrams from 0 to 31 left to right (MSB to LSB). The PDP-11 manuals numbered the bits in their diagrams from 15 to 0 left to right (MSB to LSB). So, if you wrote the bytes backwards (Right to Left) in diagrams it all came out the same, this was just an illusion caused by a stupid notation in the manuals. This turned out to be wrong. I had to come to terms on my own with an alien (to me) way of representing numbers in a computer's memory.

I continued on the project and took over all aspects of this cross assembler. I learned about relocating loader (link editor) inputs and other aspects of interfacing an executable image with an OS. This assembler went into heavy use by the project and gave good service.

The Army (1971 .. 1973)

I graduated in May of 1971. I had a low number in the Vietnam draft lottery, and was now eligible for the draft. I was ordered to take the physical exam and passed. At the time there was talk of suspending the draft. There was a political fight between Nixon and the senate. What it meant to me was I could not make any plans. I did not want to start something that might be interrupted.

That summer I implemented Conway's game of 'Life' on a PDP-9 with an attached vector graphic display. My roommate had access to this machine. There was no disk, just 16K of 18-bit words, and a paper tape reader. But it had this awesome vector graphics display. I learned the graphics commands and OS and wrote a Life simulation. It used the light pen to position the pieces. The first version was too slow due to the way I manipulated the pieces as bits packed into the machine's words. I made a small ad-hoc speed up modification and got good results.

The moral was: in the tradeoff between simple robust design and performance, often the simple design is OK. Performance either never becomes an issue, or can be addressed by paying attention to a few aspects of an inner loop. "Often" does not mean "Always". Several times in my career I would face the exact opposite situation, and need to totally scrap the first design in favor of a much more complex design to get essential performance. However, I saved a lot of work over the years by trying the simple first.

At the end of the summer my lease was up, so I went home and enlisted in the Army for two years. Just to remove the great uncertainty. The draft was suspended at the time. It was later briefly reinstated then permanently stopped. Had I waited, I might never have been drafted, or been able to delay things till the draft was scrapped. I did not know this at the time and have no regrets.

On the enlistment form I put every buzzword possible about computers, assembly language, practical experience, etc. I lucked out big time. After basic training my platoon was assigned to some southern fort for advanced infantry training and shipment to Vietnam, but I got orders to go directly to NORAD headquarters in Colorado Springs and work for the Army Air Defense Command.

I worked in the War Games section. My bosses were civilians. The computer was a CDC 6600. The program was a large Monte Carlo simulator. My job was to maintain OP-POP (Optimal Population targeting). This FORTRAN program managed a large database of US population arranged by geographic coordinates. The program knew how to estimate the accuracy and damage of various atomic bombs attached to various ICMBs. I was totally amazed by the accuracy assumptions.

A typical job request was: target X number of missiles each with Y type bombs. Where should they be aimed to destroy the most US citizens? The program would spit out longitude and latitude coordinates in a specific target sequence.

Reading other's code

The biggest challenge of this job was to read and understand a truly large program that I did not design or write. Needless to say, there was no documentation of the internal design, and the prior owner was gone. I started reading the listing. There was a printed listing, and a card deck. No word search. No cross reference. As I learned the code, I saw the de-facto design, and started to see ways to simplify and improve it. I started to talk about this. I was proud of myself that I could figure out the original design, and see improvements. I started to talk about the deficiencies in the program as I had inherited it.

I was lucky. One of the other enlisted guys who had been there a while asked if I would go for a walk with him during lunch. He calmly and matter of factly told me that the prior owner was a real nice person that everyone had liked, and I was acting like a big jerk with my comments. I was very chagrined. I had no intention of running the other person down. It was all about me: After great effort I was able to see the design and improvements. I changed my behavior, but never forgot the chagrin. Not all jerks are really jerks; some are just insensitive and stupid. Lucky I was put wise.

The HP-35

We used spherical trigonometry a lot in this job. Calculating distances, azimuths. We had a desktop HP calculator. It used RPN and displayed a little stack on its screen. Then the HP-35 was released. I immediately grabbed $450 (a ton of money for me at that time) and drove to a Hewlett-Packard office in Denver and bought one of the first HP-35s made. I was in heaven. I used it a lot on the job. Word got around. I had Army Majors and Captains come up to me and say: "C.. c.. can I like, borrow it for a few hours ??" Sure, no problem.

I currently own the original HP-35, an HP-15c, an HP-12c, and an HP-48GX all of which still work.. For each one I spent weeks with the manuals mastering all aspects of their operation. I have seldom needed trigonometry or any functions beyond add, subtract, multiply, or divide after this Army job.

Summer Job

I was discharged from the Army in the spring of 1973. I had arranged to start working on a Master's degree in Computer, Information, and Control Engineering starting in the fall of 1973. Meantime, I got a summer job in Colorado Springs working for a small company on the PDP-8. The application was a radio station advertising database. Glass teletypes were used to enter and display information. My boss described in general terms what the data entry needed to do.

This was another large, difficult but fun project. I set out with legal pads and wrote reams of PDP-8 assembly code. I typed it all in and got it running. I was very proud. I figured I had done a lot of really good work. I had some slick user interface features to make data entry easy. Demo time. The demo was to an older guy I had never met before. Someone from 'marketing'. I proudly did the demo, which worked well. The guy just said: "Do you have any idea how radio advertising is sold?"

Er, no. So what? I did not say that, and the guy was polite. He mentioned a few things about horizontal and vertical time blocks. Spots. Stuff I had never heard of. My boss was impressed with my work, but the reaction of the marketing guy took the wind out of my sails. I could take no joy in the technical achievement, because I now knew it was not what was needed. I am so glad this happened so early in my career. I found out directly and personally that such a thing as 'marketing' existed before I could learn the typical attitude that computer program implementers have toward marketing. I only talked to the guy for at most an hour. He was kind enough to sketch out what a useful solution should do. He was totally un-impressed with my work.

The results of the conversation made a permanent and deep impression on me. I was lucky to be exposed to this situation at the very beginning of my career. Just as important, I was able to talk to this marketing guy directly, un-filtered by my boss. Here was this guy from another, non-technical part of the company who judged my work on criteria I had never heard of.

At the time, I did not think to question why I had not met this guy at the start of the project. My boss in R&D was happy with my work, but this other guy was not. I felt no personal sense of failure because my boss was happy, but I considered the effort "to have failed" (passive voice intentional)

Regardless, my boss liked my work and wanted me to stay on in the fall. He went to a lot of effort to persuade me. I was tempted, but stuck to the plan. Back to school for a Master's on the GI bill.

Master's Degree (1973 .. 1974)

My attitude was: get the ticket punched as quickly and as easily as possible. There was Computer Science, or Computer, Information, and Control Engineering (CICE). Computer Science had a lot of prestige. It was very theoretical. Turing machines. Non-deterministic automata. Ugh. CICE had less prestige, and a bunch of requirements for analog control systems that I did not care about. I chose CICE as the lesser of the evils. I just wanted a Masters, any old Masters. As it turned out, in my career as a programmer this degree did not matter one bit till 20 years later when I applied for a job at a Fortune 500 company. At that time, even though the degree was 20 years old and obsolete, it magically un-locked the door to employment and advancement.

I paid little attention to the classes. I was working part time again for some of the same people that employed me to work on the PDP-11 cross assembler. They had formed a very small company to work on a new database product, but were taking in any old consulting work they could get to bring in cash money. That is where I came in. They wanted me to write more cross-assemblers. This time running on the XDS-940 and the Data General Nova. This time I needed to implement them so that they were compatible with the original native assemblers. A good living.

I got my Master's degree in December of 1974, and married in March of 1975. The part time job became full time. The company wanted me to work on an embedded system to diagnose why tank motors would not start. There was already someone working on this, but I was to help. I did not talk to this guy, but soon found out that they wanted to cut this guy out, and have me complete the work. I thought that was sleazy. Also, I was not sure the system design would work. Too complex for the hardware available. Anyway, I decided to get a "real" job.

A "Real" job (1975 .. 1976)

No problem, I'll just call the guys in Colorado Springs. This was in the middle of a fairly big recession. The guy in Colorado Springs was so sorry, but absolutely nothing was available. Business was terrible. Lots of problems. Colorado Springs especially hard hit. Hot shot young programmer meets the business cycle? Not really this time. That lesson was delayed for 20 years.

I sent out 50 resumes. I got two interviews: Bell Labs in New Jersey, and a Burroughs site in Southern California. The Bell labs interview was very structured. They flew me out. Limo at the airport. Full day schedule. Motel stay. They soon offered me a job in a group working on a large IBM assembly language application. The interview was full of talk about "egoless programming", and "Structured walk-throughs". This talk made my blood run cold. I nodded and smiled. The offer was very good.

Meantime, the Burroughs interview was less formal. I needed to get myself to California on my own. We had scheduled a vacation out there to visit my uncle in-law. The borrowed car made me half hour late to the interview. I told them I had an offer back in New Jersey, so if they were to make an offer, it needed to be during my vacation. They offered less money to work on a COBOL application. COBOL ! Yuck !

I called back the same day and accepted the California offer. My wife never returned to Ann Arbor. I flew back and moved our apartment out to Santa Ana a month later. There were lots of conflicting factors in this decision, but one of the big ones was "Egoless programming". My ego was heavily into all programming I did, and to have to start and continue a job with so basic a lie seemed like an impossible thing for me to do. A second factor was California vs. New Jersey.

Books talked about how programming needed to "grow up" and become professional. The great Bell Labs obviously wanted "grown up" programmers. At the time, I felt like a child about having my ego in my programs. Later on, this guilt went away. The talk about "Egoless programming" died down some, but never went away. The computer is a tabula rasa. The programmer is like an author of novels, faced with a blank sheet of paper. There are countless effective ways to solve any given problem. A specific design is just as much an act of creation as writing a story. If this is not ego, then I don't know what is.

Of course, the paper is never entirely blank. The more preexisting environment that exists, the more like an engineer the programmer needs to be. As time goes on, one would expect that the art would be driven out of programming as more and more preexisting techniques are re-used. Unfortunately for this view, the pace of progress in computer design keeps increasing, and best techniques keep changing. Finally, reading history shows that there is ego even in something as seemingly cut and dried as civil engineering. (e.g. bridge building)

COBOL programmer

First day on the job working for the big corporation in California. I did not see anyone who interviewed me. My new boss was someone I had never spoken to. He did not seem all that excited to see me. At that time I did not drink much coffee, but to make conversation I asked where the coffee was. Next thing I knew I was in charge of the office coffee pool. Collecting dues, buying coffee, keeping the coffee area in shape.

The work was better than I thought it would be. They used COBOL because the Burroughs Medium system was a COBOL machine. It worked with decimal data. You could not write a decent 'C' compiler for this machine. What would 'shift left 3', or 'exclusive or' mean to a decimal number ? Something could be found for it to mean, but this was a native COBOL computer. In a way, its numbers were closer to everyday numbers than all other computers I had used so far.

The application was one of the most complex I ever worked on. It was a program generator. It read in a specification for a report against a database. This specification was in a language similar to SQL. The database specifications were obtained directly from one of several Burroughs databases. The application would then create a COBOL program that when executed would create the desired report. One of the more clever parts of this application was in the automatic output formatting. Many heuristics were used so the resulting report looked good without the user needing to do any format specification.

The code for this application was written in a macro like language interspersed with COBOL snippets. The macro language featured subroutines, looping, conditionals. The macro interpreter was itself a COBOL program. This was systems programming in COBOL. The only traditional business COBOL type program involved was the ultimate report program that was the result of the process.

The team consisted of six or so people including a boss. We all sat at desks in the same room. My initial assignment was 'dates'. I was working at one quarter speed from prior efforts. The rest of the time was taken up in talk. Debates on style. Debates on the best algorithm. My boss thought I was too clever with the code. He wanted more 'maintainable' code. I had a hard time taking this seriously. The code spoke for itself. Anyone could read it and see what was going on.

We also had lots of debates on 'structured programming'. There were guest lecturers. Structured COBOL, what was it? Well we all had opinions, and debated them earnestly. The discussions were collegial. It was hard for me to relate them to my job, because we had this massive operational, pre-existing code base that did not conform. My boss was of the definite opinion that the entire code base could be migrated over time to a new design and coding style. I strongly disagreed. We debated this point often.

All of my limited experience rebelled against messing with working code except to change specific functionality. Whenever I had done this, often it got worse before it got better. If you were going to have to debug the code again, why not start over with a radically different (and better) design? In my opinion, code is like a living thing. Once it is born, or starts into production, it is “alive”. It must constantly stay alive. There is a natural way for it to grow and develop new functionality all the while “staying alive”. But major design changes are like surgery: dangerous. After some surgery, parts of the code can die and need to be amputated.

Most of the time, the best course of action is to let a working program grow old gracefully, all the while a separate effort is nurturing a new embryo that will start out with a new design and new possibilities for rapid growth.

In many ways the working environment was a throwback to my undergraduate days. The entire code base was on punch cards. Merging in a change was a literal physical merge. At one point the company wanted us to code on special sheets so the keypunching could be sent out. What a disaster. I had evolved into an incredibly accurate keypuncher, but I was not so efficient at proof-reading. Fortunately, they did not insist.

Programming as a Hobby

The slow pace of actual program design and development caused me to take up programming as a hobby. I had read a description of ‘pentominoes’ which were 12 shapes that could be fit together like a puzzle. I wrote a program that generated solutions to this puzzle. I used the machine at work, and wrote in COBOL. A stack based backtracking algorithm in COBOL. Several people at work knew about this. I kept it low key and there was no official notice or trouble.

I used the computer at work because there was no other way. That would change in a very few years when the micro computer revolution hit. Once I got my first personal computer (An IMSAI 8080 in 1977) I never used resources from work again.

I have continued to program as one of my hobbies ever since this. The level of activity is in inverse proportion to the amount of design and development I was doing at work. I seem to need to maintain a constant level of effort designing and implementing new computer programs. The pentomino program has had many implementations in many languages over the next 35 years. Most recently as a MS-Windows / C++ application.

Moving on

After what seemed like an entire career, but was really only one and a half years, I quit and moved onto what became my first real career. I was called in for my first performance evaluation. The man said we really like you. You have a great future here. You get the largest raise possible: 6%. Next year you can get the same, or even better if the guidelines are revised. Somehow I found out that the minimum raise was 3%.

I was frustrated at the slow pace, endless academic debate, and I was not learning anything new about computers or programming. Now I find the margin between a star and the minimum was 3%. The future at this shop was all too easy to imagine. I felt confined. I thought of going back for my PhD like all of my old roommates were doing. I had no love for the academic aspects of computer science. I liked the actual implementation. I wanted to talk to marketing, design, implement, debug, see the result in active use. Have users like the result.

So I answered a two line small ad in the classifieds: "Wanted Data General Programmer". I was not aware of it, but the recession was over. Two weeks later I was back doing assembly language programming for a startup. Besides the handful of founders, I was their first employee.

Career Number One (1977 .. 1980)

Small Startup

This startup was going to calculate automobile insurance rates for independent insurance agents hooked up to a state wide network. The computer used was a DG Eclipse. This was a successor to the Nova. We started with 64KB memory (all that can be addressed with a 16 bit word). We had 10MB of disk space. The operating system was RDOS, which provided access to files on the disk, and two multi threaded processes.

The network consisted of "smart" terminals hooked up to leased telephone lines. The terminals supported a multi-drop polled bi-sync protocol at 2400 baud. We put about 20 of these terminals on one line. We transmitted an application form to the screen, which the user filled out and transmitted back. The system then extracted the data, rated the application for 20 different insurance companies, and transmitted the sorted results back.

Programming Environment

This was all programmed in assembly language. A weird mix of systems and business programming. The systems challenge was to support as many terminals as possible on an Eclipse computer. The business challenge was to support as many different insurance companies as possible. The methods of rating policies were varied. The rates kept changing. We only had access to the published rate tables, no inside info.

The work environment was a line editor on a dumb terminal. Initially, access to a terminal was limited, so the method of writing out lots of code, then typing it all in was still necessary. Debugging was a mixture of analyzing core dumps, and a primitive interactive debugger. This was a multi-threaded application. Since there was only one process and one memory space available, the program used threads dynamically to buffer the communications and application work. Other threads were created and destroyed as the work load waxed and waned. In this type of environment, the core dump was the main tool. Breakpoints were seldom useful, because they totally changed the interaction among the threads. We invested heavily in custom core dump formatters and interpreters.

One of the founders had written the initial code. It was not yet done when I came on. I set to work learning how it all worked. I found an error while reading the code and my experience in the Army had taught me how to react. I went to the chief programmer and was very deferential about a possible bug. He investigated, and thanked me for finding it. We got off on the right foot, and I was accepted as an equal partner in future design discussions.

There were tons of design and work to do. We got all of the initial required applications working. We were able to stay ahead of sales and installation in terms of processing the load.

Marketing

I started to see a pattern in how the business was run. The salesmen would come back and say "We need this new feature X". "I can't sell what we got, but I could sell Y new units if we could get feature X in there." Different salesmen each had a different feature X. All of this would get prioritized, and we worked at speed to get it done. Sales were OK, the company took off. It did not fly too high, but did solid business.

I was able to talk candidly with some of the salesmen. I would challenge the need for feature X. "Did one customer just mention it in passing? Was it part of any larger strategy?" In turn they would ask: "How hard can this be to put in? It is a small change from what you have now".

Later on, one of the best salesmen was promoted to "Marketing". Is marketing more than just the boss of all salesmen? Is marketing just a clearinghouse so all the salesmen's requests can be funneled to R&D?

I heard the salesmen sometimes talk about their customers. "The way this guy does business, he really does not have a big need for the unit, he just wants it out there to impress his customers." Or, "This guy is our ideal customer, and he has really given this a lot of thought, I think his suggestion is good". Or, "That feature he wants is baloney, he is really too cheap to buy a unit". Sometimes the salesmen would talk about the competition. There was no direct competition, but there were alternatives for getting roughly the same service.

For my part, I would go into the technical details of what was needed to provide feature X, Y, or Z. I doubt they understood all of what I was saying, but it was more useful to them than saying "No". I fell into a pattern of discussion by saying "Yes, we can do that, but ..." I would then launch into a long sad technical story. Sometimes I was able to say: "Hmm, yes we can do that, in fact we can easily do that plus this as well; I'll get right on it."

Many of these conversations allowed each of us to see the other's real problems and limitations. I came to think that the role of marketing was to take the "other" side of these types of conversations with R&D. Not to just whine for whatever feature the last customer asked for.

The relationship between R&D and Marketing can be adversarial. This does not mean that the people involved need to mis-trust each other. Indeed, each side needs to respect the other. But the goals are different, and both sides need advocates who will represent the unique viewpoint of their side. Only then can the ensuing negotiation arrive at an optimal solution for the business as a whole.

Later in my career, at a Fortune 500 company, management would beat up the R&D lab by saying "The Customer is Always Right". This was used as a trump card, to stop further discussion. Sometimes a customer does not know what he wants. Sometimes a product is different enough to require the customer to change their operation. If the gains for doing this are great, then often the new product eventually becomes a new standard imitated by competitors. Is the customer's initial "No, I don't need that feature" Right?

Cool Projects

Time was also set aside for improvements in processing efficiency. One exciting project I got to do was to move all of the communications off onto a data concentrator board with its own processor. The company sold the hardware, but there was absolutely zero programming support. So I got to write a little multi-thread monitor program that mimicked the main processor's RDOS and turn all of the per-character interrupts into block DMA transfers.

Another exciting project was memory management. You could install more memory than the 64KB that could be directly addressed. The processor had memory map registers that allowed portions of memory to be mapped in or out of the 64K accessible window. As par for the course, the OS did not yet support this. So I got the job of allowing the application to access this memory without the OS being aware of it. We implemented a crude code paging system that eliminated disk overlays. Also the communication buffers could be stuffed in this area.

I was in heaven. I was on the job 24x7. If I was not at the office, I was thinking about it.

Operation

We soon had to hire an operator to manage the operation. We had a growing on-line statewide network. Phone lines would go down, terminals would not work. Occasionally the computer application would crash. The flow of problems was continual, but most of the problems were routine, and easily handled.

We programmers would get involved in these problems whenever any non-routine situation came up. In self-defense we would build features into the system's operator interface that allowed the operator to figure out as much as possible on their own. Every once in a while the operator would mis-use the interface and cause the system to crash. They were so apologetic. They took all blame. They never complained about a difficult user interface.

One of the biggest changes over my career has been the change in the relationship between programmer and user. With only 64K Bytes of RAM and a 16 bit CPU, all resources were needed for the application. User interface design concentrated on providing needed options with the minimal use of resources. The users understood this, and never complained. They took pride in mastering the sometimes arcane user interfaces needed to control the awesome power of the computer. Mistakes were their fault. The programmer who fixed the resulting mess was a hero.

As the available computer power increased, it was used to make the user interface more elaborate. The great advance here was the GUI. I was always amazed when I realized that a 32bit CPU with 16MB RAM and full color screen with 1024 x 768 pixels was a rather minimum configuration for simple GUI applications. In my undergrad days, the central campus computer was a 32 bit CPU with 8MB.

Users started blaming the programmer when they made mistakes. We were no longer heroes. We were on the defensive. Any confusion in how to operate a computer was a user interface design error. People expected user interfaces to do much more than they ever could.

Every once in a while the problem was the system itself. Then the tensions between operator and programmer rose. We took over the computer. Poked around, talked among ourselves. Finally we would walk away and say over our shoulder, OK you can re-boot. From the operator's point of view the system was down, the phones would start to ring and we seemed to be so blasé , slow and un-informative. Finally we would say "re-boot", which was a chore. "Will it happen again ?" "Um... don't know." Sometimes we would run experimental code which caused lots of deliberate crashes. (So we could get productive core dumps). Hard to explain to the operators.

By and large the system worked very well. Although assembly language is not inherently a forgiving language to work in, we were very, very careful, and never even began to think about stinting on quality to meet schedule. I never remember any pressure about schedule. "When will feature X be done ?" "Um.. don't know, maybe Friday, maybe not." "I told the customer it would be ready Friday." "Oh ? Wow ! Too bad, it won't."

In retrospect, I think we got away with this attitude because lots of stuff got done quickly at high quality, and it was obvious we were all happily working hard. What can I say ? We were good. In my ignorance it never occurred to me that the owner could have tried to speed things up.

Pascal

We finally realized we needed to get away from assembly language for the actual insurance rating portion of the system. We did not have the space to store all of the rates. There were so many companies, that the rates were always changing for one of them or another. We generated the rates using home grown algorithms from a minimum of stored data. Sometimes the rate change was a simple change in one of the stored numbers. Sometimes we needed to change a compiled-in number. Sometimes an algorithm needed to be changed.

The application needed to expand from the initial handful of screens to many more specialized screens. We made this as simple as possible to do in the code, but it needed someone who knew Eclipse assembly language. We decided to embed a Pascal interpreter into the system. The decision to use Pascal was influenced by the existence of UCSD Pascal. I drove to San Diego and got the documentation packet. Ultimately, for us to use this system we would have had to pay big (for us) bucks to UCSD, and then do all the adaptation work ourselves.

Instead, we got a free tape of the public domain Pascal distribution. This included the compiler, interpreter, internals documentation and test cases. It ran on a CDC 6600. It was my job to make this run on the

Eclipse and embed an interpreter into our system. We needed to extend the language to hook into our screen send and receive sub-system.

The listing of the Pascal compiler was 6 inches thick. It was written in the best possible Pascal by N. Wirth's project. What a learning experience that was. Structured programming as taught by the master himself. I fell in love with Pascal. At that time the book *Algorithms + Data Structures = Programs* by Wirth came out. That book was a real education for me.

Creating an interpreter that ran on our 16-bit Eclipse was relatively easy, because the definition of the P-Codes was a given. Converting the output of the compiler to my interpreter's made up binary code was an exercise in writing a cross assembler, something I had done five or six times before. This project turned out well. We eventually had four or five programmers writing Pascal code which ran on our rating system.

Amusing Story

One of the applications we ran was an automatic driver record look-up with the DMV. Insurance agents would fill out electronic forms with an applicant's name and driver's license number and we would consolidate a day's worth of requests onto a 9-track tape and submit it to the DMV. The next morning we would take the result 9-track tape and format them into official looking driver records and transmit them back to the agents.

I was worried, because the agent who received the form could very easily alter the results on the screen prior to printing it out. I could not get any of my co-workers to feel the risk. I went ahead and added a 16 digit checksum in the lower right corner of the transmitted form. This checksum coded for the number of accidents, drunk driving, and other felonies from the driving record. Everyone thought I was obsessive, but they allowed it to stand. I wrote a Pascal program to convert any checksum back into a list of felonies. Users were told it was a control code, and not to mess with it.

Twenty years later, I was told the story of a driver who had an accident that the insurance company would not pay. The company said he got the insurance by fraud, because he had all these drunken driving arrests. The insurance agent showed them our report, which showed a clean driving record, and said it was our fault. My old company remembered my decoder program, and typed in the checksum from that old clean driving record. Out prints several drunk driving arrests. The agent had altered the record so he could write the insurance and blame us if it was ever necessary. Opps.

Boss Man

More programmers and greatly expanded application functionality required another level of management. The original founding programmer never wanted anything to do with this. One of my good friends got the job, and managed the move of all computer equipment from our original quarters to a brand new building. What a chore, dealing with specifications, Phone Company, contractors. A half year later he left for Northern California.

I was asked if I wanted to be in charge of the programmers. I said "sure". I gave no thought to what this job entailed beyond the fact that now everyone would have to do what I said. Sort of like a High School club. I got along with everyone, this would be no sweat.

Hiring

I was involved in interviews. Many people were obviously un-qualified. Others talked a great game. Looked you in the eye and said all of the right things. Others were difficult to figure out. No one seemed to have just the right mix of experience, but we desperately needed to hire. So we hired the best of the lot we interviewed. I assumed they would all be like me. Dig in, find out about it all. Jump to do what needed to be done. It was not like that. Some had more initiative than others. Some required detailed instructions. Some shirked and did very little.

I made no effort to inspire or lead. I would discuss design and goals with them, but if they would not push back with knowledge and conviction, I would end the discussion with "Just do it this way". I was expecting to relate with everyone the same way I had related with the founding programmer, and there was no way they could. I was not aware of any of this. By and large people seemed content. Work was getting done.

Firing

Except for one guy. I was very irritated with this guy. He talked a great game, but never did anything. He had good reasons for why stuff did not get done. Confusing specifications. Changing requirements. Whatever. I did not take any of these reasons seriously, and felt no need to address any of these excuses. I just wanted to get rid of him. My boss said OK. So I gave him a very limited specific task, and asked him when he would have it done. On that day I asked about the results. It was not complete, and I ignored whatever he said. The next day I called him into my office, handed him a letter of resignation and asked him to sign it.

He was so shocked that he signed it. This was in the days when you could walk across the street and get a 20% raise any time you wanted to. Looking back on this from 25 years later I blush with embarrassment. What a colossal asshole I was. In my defense, I had no malice. This guy was like a malfunctioning code fragment. Debugging was hard, so it needed to be re-written. Problem solved. I never wanted to get involved with the programmers as people. Only as subroutines in a larger code base. I imagine there were many other bosses like me in small companies at that time. If I did that stunt today, I and the company would be sued so fast my head would spin. I will have much more to say about human interactions in the programming world later in this book

Collaboration

I developed a good professional relationship with two of the other programmers. We would discuss design problems with each other. We would listen, and ask questions. This kind of active listening took time and effort, but we were happy to do it because the favor would be returned.

By discussing ideas with another, you could get quick validation, or find potential problems with less effort. When challenged with: "Yea, OK, but then what about the effect on this other situation" you were put on the spot and refined or abandoned your idea.

The level of abstraction in these discussions would quickly range all over the gamut from low level details, to the highest level principles. Many times some very stupid things would be said, but no one felt bad about it. Sometimes, just being forced to speak an idea out loud was enough feedback, and the other guy never had so say a word.

A sort of positive dynamic was at work here: Give away ideas freely. If they work out well, the recipient will consciously or un-consciously associate the success with you. They would return respect and good will. Many times it was not possible to attribute the resulting design with any specific person. At the time I thought this was a common, natural way for design work to be done.

Hobby

Somehow during all of this I found time to put together an IMSAI 8080 kit computer. I got 8KB of memory for it. I built it and wrote a Z-80 cross assembler for it that ran on the Eclipse at work. Output was a paper tape. One of the older Eclipses at work had a paper tape punch.. The main program I got running on it was the Pentomino solver. It was fun to watch the trial solutions flicker in the direct-map video memory. The drawback was there was no hardcopy output. I needed to copy the solutions it found off the screen by hand.

Finances

I made a good wage, but nothing excessive. I had 1000 shares of stock, but had no idea of what it was worth. The capital structure of the company was not talked about. There was one new investor who came in midway during my tenure there. I gathered he bought needed equipment and paid debts. We were all aware that the company needed any cash it could come up with to stay alive.

All was well till my first child was born. Months later, all of the doctors called up and said that my health insurance was not paying on the claim. I called up the insurance company, who said "yea, we have these claims but we won't pay them because the premium has not been paid".

I walked across the hall to the book keeper, a nice older lady, who got this sad expression on her face. No we did not pay the premium. I called the insurance company back and asked what they would have paid out. They give me a figure, and I asked the owner for the money. I eventually got it. I do not recall being outraged, or very worried. I was more concerned for the company than for myself. I sold my IMSAI to someone deluded he was going to automate his office, and paid the doctors with the proceeds.

I had one troublesome discussion with my boss. They had hired a guy to supply long term planning. He was a good talker, but not a programmer. I found out they were paying him a lot more than me, so I asked why. My boss said that we cannot pay you that much, it would be too large a raise, percentage wise. I said I could get that much if I walked across the street. He agreed. So where is the sense in that? No answer, except that we really, really like the job you are doing. At the time I was irritated, but did not quit. This episode provided the first crack in my un-questioning thralldom to the company's fortune. The guy they hired never contributed much to the company so far as I could tell.

The company never became really successful, and it never went bankrupt. It was sold several times. The applications continued to run. New ones were added. The founding programmer stayed on for 20 years. I know some of the code I wrote there was running twenty years later. I sold the stock back to the company for $1000. I don't think it was ever worth more. No one got rich. But I learned a lot and had great fun.

I left after 4 years. Basically, I was bored. Bossing was just an irritation. No new technical challenges were in the immediate future. My thralldom was broken. Time to move on. Looking back, it is amazing how much I learned and got done in those four years. I came to think of it as my first career.

Interlude (1981 .. 1982)

Crazy

My good friend, who was the programmer's boss before me, called me up and offered a job in Northern California doing DG Eclipse work for a Gold trader. This was during the time the price of Gold ran up to $800/oz. The guy was expanding into other areas like tax shelters.

I was astonished to learn how futures trading worked. How a little bit of margin money could control lots of potential profits (or losses). This guy was able to obtain loans from major respected banks for the margin money. This was a twice leveraged game of out-guessing other sharp traders in real time. Very nerve-wracking. The company owner was consistently successful at this, but wanted to expand into less risky forms of business.

My project was to design and implement an order processing system for financial transactions. I forget the language (PL/1 ?), but it was not assembly language.

I was ready to demo a prototype, but the owner never saw it. He changed direction, and was no longer interested in that project. There was great confusion and little specific direction set. The guy actually ranted and raved. I was the last hired of four or five other programmers. There was no collaboration like I was used to. The chaotic environment seemed to foster an 'everyone for themself' attitude. There was no marketing or customers, just an unstable owner.

I quit after only 5 months. I felt bad for my friend, who was my boss. He understood my reasons, but he said I should stay on at least till

December because of the fantastic bonus. Apparently big year-end bonuses were a tradition in the financial world. Especially if the owner was erratic and needed to buy loyalty. I didn't care about money, I left anyway.

Sure enough, my friend later told me about the huge year-end bonus I had missed. I had not even a flicker of regret.

San Francisco

I forget how I found my next job, most likely from my friend and former boss. It was a small payroll processing firm in the financial district of San Francisco. This guy was taking in payroll processing for small and medium firms. He was running COBOL on old 16 bit IBM computers. The computers were no longer made, and he wanted to upgrade to Data General Eclipse computers. There was a COBOL available for the Eclipse, but the heart of his operation was the ISAM database that ran on the old IBM computers.

My project was to implement a database on the Eclipse that was functionally compatible with the old database. Then all of the COBOL programs could be converted to run on the Eclipse. Other than that specification, all was up to me. Once again, there was no marketing or customer, just the owner. But this guy was a stable successful businessman. I got to work with joy.

Environment

The Data General AOS system provided for traditional batch jobs, printer queues, and online sessions using dumb ASCII glass teletype like terminals. The system supported user accounts with passwords, a fancy file system with access control, the notion of super-user with many executive functions. The programming model was based on running many processes, each of which had access to file mapped virtual memory, sharing of memory between processes. Each process also fully supported multiple threads and inter-process communication. Up to that point, I had never programmed in a richer environment. UNIX finally achieved parity in the late 1990s.

I had always assumed that the success of a technical product was directly related to its technical merit. The two early counter examples in my career were Data General's AOS operating system, and the Motorola 68000 CPU chip. Did AOS fail because of stupid marketing by Data General? Poor networking support? Did fashion (open OS vs. closed OS) have a part? Did the M68000 fail because the Intel 8086 was used in the IBM PC? I lost so much productivity to the segmented memory model of the Intel chip; I wanted to know why I was forced to work with this inferior CPU, when there was a better one available? I started reading business histories and business magazines.

By now the programming environment included a screen editor. An entire screen of text could be displayed on a dumb glass teletype, and edited using the cursor keys, function keys, and control characters. I did not use any source versioning or control system.

Commuting

One aspect of this job was the commute. The job was in the financial district of San Francisco, and our family lived in Sonoma County. There was a commuter bus that went from my town directly to a block from work with no stops in between. The commute was an average of three hours (one hour in the morning and two hours in the evening) each day. Best was two and a half, worst was four hours. Well, worst was getting stuck in San Francisco and sleeping on a couch in the office.

I consciously decided that it was best to pick a good place to live, then find work near there. That was a part of my reason for the move from Costa Mesa to Sonoma County. I was lucky there was a good commuter system from Sonoma County to San Francisco. I was un-lucky that the commuter system did not extend further down the peninsula to Silicon Valley. When the BART (Bay Area Rapid Transit) was setup, Marin (and therefore Sonoma) county opted out. Although it was possible to commute to San Francisco, continuing on down the peninsula was not practicable. Thus, while Sonoma County was an ideal place to raise a family, high tech job opportunities were more limited.

Later on, during a bout of recession and un-employment I came to see that I had got it backwards. Pick a good place to live, then find work is a luxury. Reality was: Get a job, and then find the best place to live that you can.

I ended up doing this 3 hour (round trip) commute daily for 8 years. The commute provided a natural cycle in my work. It encouraged bankers hours. The commute bus did not run on the weekend. My inclination was to get my work done during normal hours anyway. It was easy to quit for the day and pick up the next morning refreshed. (Can't stay, got to catch the bus). The office was for working. Socializing more than just the minimum might force me to work on the weekend. I came to think of all non-essential activity at work as effectively being weekend work, and I hated working weekends. Since I was averaging 15 hours a week on the bus, on top of 45 hours of work a week, I came to think of my weekends as inviolate.

Project

I used assembly language to write a multi-threaded database server process that used Inter Process Communication to service any number of client COBOL processes. Compatibility with the older database only constrained the COBOL interface on the client side. This was a wide open design and implementation problem. The main issue was performance and ability to support a large enough database. Also needed was a universal database browser/editor. This was an assembly language application that parsed COBOL data base specifications, accessed the DB server, then displayed screens of data using the COBOL names for the fields.

I got along well with the owner. We had many discussions on the needed performance and internal design. The client/server approach was new to him, and he was skeptical of my decision to put user data and index data in the same file. He was unfamiliar with using a memory map to blur the distinction between data in a file and data in memory. I convinced him this would all work well.

On the other hand, I had never heard of traditional business data processing techniques. He wanted to know how fast this database could process a transaction file and lookup details in a master file. After some discussion, I said it was related to the disk latency. Each lookup in the master file was a random read, and no matter how efficient or lightly loaded the system was it needed to wait for the disk. He then described a traditional sort / merge where both transaction file and master detail file were sorted on the same key and processed sequentially together. There the limit in a lightly loaded system was the disk channel DMA speed. I had never thought this way.

Hobby

I had sold my IMSAI, but still had a strong need for a home computer. Just after moving to Northern California, I bought a used DG Nova from a DG salesman I knew. This baby had 10MB disk, 64 KB core memory, and the optional 16 bit Multiply/Divide unit. It lived in an industrial rack and was the size and weight of a heavy duty refrigerator. I bought and assembled a Heath Kit H-19 glass teletype and I was in business.

I got the PASCAL system I had written in Southern California up and running. I was ready. For what? I never got any real applications running. I had fun bringing the machine up, but never had much time to use it. I eventually sold it to someone in desperate need of spare parts, and escaped with only a minimal financial loss. My next five years were home computer free.

Change in Plans

The project was completed, and worked well. I had many test cases, and ran performance tests and capacity tests. In retrospect, I now realize I did not run crash tests, but it didn't matter...

The owner had gotten a good deal on a lot of old used IBM computers. He now figured that with this spare part inventory, he was safe in not converting. Although the database was done, all of the old COBOL programs still needed conversion to the Eclipse. He canceled my project. He tried to convince me that his new plans were just as exciting. But they were not. One of his salesmen told me about a small bond broker / investment manager down the street that needed a programmer. I jumped ship.

My criteria for finding a new job were based on the technical work to be done. I went after opportunities to learn new areas of technology. I wanted to avoid narrow specialization. Jack of all trades, and a master of a few. In retrospect, I also sub-consciously wanted good professional relationships with peers at work.

Career Number Two (1982 .. 1988)

My new job was with a very small investment advisor and bond brokerage that occupied two floors in a building on Montgomery Street across from the TransAmerica Pyramid. The investment advisor managed some pension funds and portions of select rich people's wealth. The brokerage operation traded mostly in bonds, but also some stocks. There was a small amount of profitable speculative trading on the firm's own account.

I was hired to be the programmer. Everyone hired into the firm wanted to get into the trading operation, where millions could be made. I saw what this entailed (Very good memory for numbers, lightning quick mental operations, calmness under confusion and pressure), and knew that this was everything I did not have. So I was content to do what I was hired to do.

I quickly saw I could get on very well there with the proper sort of attitude. That was the attitude of wily Greek slave bookkeeper in a rich Roman family. The Roman values the Greek highly, and treats him well, but the Greek must "know his place". The investment managers and traders existed in a network of relationships with other famous, rich, powerful individuals. Technology had absolutely zero appeal to them. They did not want to hear about my problems other than their name, and the dollar figure required to solve them. My job was to supply numbers on demand, sliced and diced to order. Sort of a number cowboy, or number plumber.

"OK, I see what you want" was all I needed to say. As long as the numbers kept flowing, life was good. After I earned their trust and respect I was allowed a few foibles and snits. In return I got a real close look at a very interesting culture. I received autonomy, interesting technical problems to solve, and state of the art equipment to solve them with. I was also rewarded financially.

I soon also saw that this was the way the business world in general thought of technologists. I came to think this view of the technologist's role was justified.

I never made the mistake of thinking these businessmen were smarter or better than me. Just richer. In some way, a little ignorance was a good thing from their perspective. What they chiefly needed was self-confidence, and too much knowledge can introduce doubt. I was not envious. I saw them do their deals and win and lose. Once you get up to a certain altitude, you can afford a dip without crashing. You can pull up and level off still high above the ground. I did not have the interest or ambition for that initial climb to altitude.

I was required to be at my desk at 6AM and wear a suit. The commuter bus ran that early because all of the San Francisco financial district operated on New York time. I needed to get up at 4:30AM. The commute was still three hours per day (round trip) on the average. I found out that a well made wool suit was very comfortable.

Unix environment

My boss was fresh out of Berkeley graduate school. For the first time, I had a boss younger than I was. He knew programming, but wanted a career in business. He had ordered one of the first SUN machines made. This unit arrived soon after I was hired. It was made of flat square bent metal. One MB RAM, a 170MB disk on the floor behind the desk. The screen was bitmapped, but it ran some third party character based UNIX. This was quickly replaced with SUN's own Berkeley based UNIX, but still in character mode only.

The editor was vi. This was a big change from the Eclipse screen editor because it used "modes". Once again I took the productivity hit as I learned a new editor. I eventually became very proficient, learning over 20% of the commands.

The language was 'C' of course. I had a bad first impression of 'C' by way of comparison to Pascal. But I soon saw that 'C' was just a sort of CPU independent assembly language. The old adage "I fell in love with Pascal, but got married to 'C'" described my state perfectly. I made all of the mistakes. Lost the usual day's work debugging a single equal sign inside an 'if()' expression and all the rest of it.

There was a debugger, but I made limited use of it. I had the entire machine to myself, and recompiles and reruns took no time at all. I discovered printf() and stderr, and became very productive.

Projects

My first job was to get some old FORTRAN based non-linear optimization code running in 'C' on the SUN. A large part of the investment management was to take a large pool of Bonds (Of which there are an almost unlimited number of variants) and match their cash flow to the needs of various pension funds. Which bonds can we buy for the least amount of money that will return the exact cash we need to pay out, and not a drop of cash wasted? My boss and his peers knew the math behind this, and I helped with the programming.

I got my first introduction to the UNIX way when I started talking about the program I needed to write to manage price files. We needed to track the closing price of several securities. My boss interrupted: "Just keep them in flat text files." I thought this was wrong. The effort to read the text, convert the prices to binary would overshadow the trivial processing we needed to do with the price data. My boss said "So what? This way we don't need a special editor program, we can just use 'vi'. We can also run other programs on the files." I said "I can whip up an editor program in a few days, and put any other functionality you may need into it easily" I argued strongly. This guy was younger than me with zero real-world programming experience.

I saw when it was time to lose the argument before he thought I was a bozo. I did it his way, but disagreed with the decision. After a while, when I began using grep, sort , and sed I finally got the UNIX text file based philosophy. I embraced it totally. I had the zeal of the converted.

Later on, I converted the Data General Eclipse based portfolio management system to 'C' on the SUN. This was a fill-in-the-blanks form based asset tracking system. A lot of knowledge about financial instruments (stocks, bonds, options, futures contracts) was built into it. They got rid of the Eclipse computer, and the Eclipse programmer left the firm. My strategy of avoiding specialization seemed to be working.

One of the main users of this portfolio tracking program was the owner of the firm. I got another lesson in customer relations. I had printed date intervals on one of the reports related to the timespan requested when the report was generated and the securities appearing on the page. The owner stopped me in the hall and said, "That date is wrong". I said "No, here, it works like this... blah, blah" The owner said. "That date is wrong". I said "Well, there is an interpretation here that gives information on the securities that matured during the interval". The owner showed some frustration: "That date is wrong". I said, "OK, yep I'll fix it". I thought long and hard about it, but I finally figured out his interpretation of that date. It was not what I thought was right or useful, but he was correct. Based on that way of looking at it, the date was wrong. Some customers are indeed right, but cannot (be bothered to) articulate why. The wise number plumber had better figure it out anyway.

In this job I first encountered a negotiating technique that was used by several people when they did not want to invest much time in the negotiation, but wanted to assure themselves that they were getting the best possible deal. I called this technique "ask for all, settle for what you can get" technique. This requires a certain aggressiveness. The negotiator never concedes any points. The negotiator may or may not listen to your offers, but never acknowledges any understanding or sympathy. Later on, they are happy with whatever you give them. They know you worked as hard as you could, and therefore they got the best deal they could have. .

Another fun project was a program trading system. One of the analysts there created a mathematical model which he said could make money trading futures contracts. I implemented the model to his specification as a program running on the SUN. He would type in the closing price of 10 or so futures contracts, and the program would spit out buy and sell orders to be executed at market open the next morning. It worked. No fantastic gains, just consistent gains. That is remarkable given the nature of futures contracts.

A book I read and profited greatly from at this time was *Software Tools* by Kernighan and Plauger. The version I got was based on FORTRAN, but the ideas were presented in structured form, and were easily adapted to 'C'.

System Administration

The initial sheet metal SUN system continued to serve, but as the company expanded, we bought several more computers. We got several rack mounted SUNs with terminal multiplex units. This allowed 8 (later 16) dumb terminals to be connected using the RS-232 Async protocol at 9600 baud.

The firm dedicated a room for this equipment. The equipment needed to be situated so visitors could see our "data center". I found myself involved in administrative duties. Setting up a backup rotation, allocating the various machines to the various programs. This was made easier by Ethernet and NFS. The SUN OS had a very good implementation of UNIX networking, and this created flexibility in how we used the machines. It was wonderful to run a program on a machine different from the one connected to the terminal, using the "rlogin" facility.

I sometimes strung terminal wire and Ethernet cable in the ceilings. I brought my soldering iron to work and made countless D25 terminal connectors, and null modems. Any computer or terminal problem was brought to my attention. I figured out the problem and fixed it if I could, or called the proper repair man.

In my role as sysadmin, I often dealt with salesmen and contractors. We were always expanding the capacity of our computers and communications. Although I ran some wire in the ceiling, most of the wire was pulled in conduit by contractors. I got to where I liked some of the contractors more than the others. I soon saw a pattern. The ones I liked listened to what I needed done, then looked me in the eye and said "Piece of Cake, I'll get right on it". I didn't think these contractors were smarter or more competent that the others, but I sure liked the feeling I got when they said that.

This was less work than it seems. My main goal was to minimize the demands on my time. To that end, things were under-utilized, and change was held to a minimum. We were always running very old versions of the SUN OS. New computers were ordered with configurations similar to the existing ones. Sometimes we needed to order expansion equipment that forced an OS roll. Those never went smoothly. Afterwards, there were inevitably minor incompatibilities with older programs. I needed to re-work stuff that used to work flawlessly, which went against my grain.

The only real fiasco I was involved in was ultimately due to the purchase of a third party memory expansion board. It took a month to finally figure this out. The production system would just panic at intervals of from every other day up to twice a day. The stated cause of the panic was a red herring. There was no correlation with anything. I suspected power, so we got a fancy power monitor. Nope. This became a fiasco because at that time, for some forgotten reason, there was no backup system capable of processing the work. We finally switched out all boards till the problem went away.

I am glad of this entire experience with system administration, because I got to see how computers behave when put into production. The developer's attitude of wanting to try each cool new thing was tempered with the knowledge that ultimately, this was not a toy and real work was expected from these machines.

Registered

The owner wanted to be able to brag about the professionalism of the staff. He decided all needed to pass the so called "Series 7" exam, and become a "registered representatives". There was an exam given to brokers who want to be licensed to sell securities to the general public. It covers a wide area from ethics, to basic knowledge of securities and markets, to exotic stuff like how margin accounts are calculated. The owner paid for an on-site tutoring course during work hours. After the course, we all went to South San Francisco and took the exam. I passed, and was duly "registered" to sell securities to the public. (Which I never did). In later years this fact was a fun conversation piece for me.

Accounting

The portfolio program kept track of investments, but the firm's bookkeeping system was manual. It was a small firm, but because it was a broker there were lots of regulatory reports. The firm was growing in terms of the number of people, and the volume of business per person was growing.

They decided to computerize the books and brokerage operation. The IBM-PC had come out, and we bought one of the first with the 10MB disk drive. Although this was used by the bookkeepers (primarily to run Lotus 123), there were no brokerage accounting programs for the PC at that time. There were general bookkeeping programs, but the person who was in charge of the firm's books (financial officer) was adverse to change. What was really wanted was a computerized system that was very close to the existing manual system in terms of account structure and reports generated.

They asked if I wanted to create an accounting system in the 'C' language to run on the SUN machines. I thought it would be an incredible challenge, and great fun, and eagerly agreed. The customer was the firm's financial officer. She was somewhat difficult to get along with, but she had a virtue I did not recognize till later: She knew exactly what she wanted. I got books on accounting. I found that double entry bookkeeping was interesting. The organization of the different category of accounts and the way any type of transaction could be broken down into debits and credits to several of these categories appealed to me.

The first step was to automate the General Ledger. My prototype lacked a key feature in the bookkeeper's eyes, but I could fix it without a major design change. This went into production and was well received. It ought to have been, because all of the features of the manual system were preserved.

The next step was to automate the trading system and back office. The requirements were interesting, because the traders could trade among themselves. In that case there was no accounting entry from the overall firm's perspective because the inventory of that security did not change. But from the trader's perspective there was definitely a trade there, and a potential paycheck. The system needed to keep the books from several different perspectives simultaneously. I was very proud of my solution to this problem.

From beginning to end, it took two years to get the system done. There was a "big bang" cutover date. I stayed in the city for several days during this time. I needed to train and support the data entry operators, support the program itself, and support the back office staff as they started using the new reports. The experience was a huge feedback loop on my original design and implementation. I welcomed it, because my ultimate motivation in programming has always been to see the results successfully used.

This system was used through three yearly cycles while I was there. Near the end of that time it was starting to suffer from performance problems. The volume of trades had increased tremendously. I was beginning to design improvements when the market crash of 1987 put a damper on trading activities.

This was the largest system I ever designed and implemented solo. In self-defense, I adapted new styles of programming. I gravitated to a style that I later found out was similar to object oriented programming. My overriding design goal was always "No trouble calls for me to respond to". I succeeded at this, things ran well.

Hiring

At some point I got some help. I was told to hire and supervise another programmer. I placed a small ad in the San Francisco paper that ran for one week. The stack of resumes was over a foot thick when I stopped even glancing at them. There were enough responses in the first two weeks to provide a dozen qualified interviews. I asked the same question of each applicant, and the answers were instructive.

I would write out the formula for the payment on a fully amortized loan, given a dollar amount, interest rate, and time period. I would say that this formula was used in a 'C' library function called 'Payment(amt, interest, time)'. Given this, I would ask how they would approach writing a function called 'Interest(amt, payment, time)'. If they started manipulating the formula, I would fairly quickly interrupt them to say that that the algebra would never work. This was a computer programming question, not a math question.

Given my early introduction to computers, you can see what I was looking for (binary search). It was amazing to me how few graduates with a degree in computers could answer this. In fact, over many years I would guess that only 5% or so ever did. I kept asking the same question, but I started to give lots of partial credit depending on how far they got, and their reaction to their failure.

I hired someone just out of college, and they started in learning the environment. They proved to be an enthusiastic, quick learner, and pitched right in.

Hobby

In 1987 the first Macintosh with a built-in hard disk drive was released. I bought one. The Mac had the same CPU chip as our SUN machines: the Motorola 68000 series. I was interested to learn all about this GUI and mouse stuff. Apple had released a superb book that documented their GUI philosophy, and also documented the API. I bought a 'C' compiler for the Macintosh, and started fooling around.

GUI programming was a lot of work for little in the way of end application results, but the programs were all very fun to run. I enjoyed writing GUI programs as hobby horses. My serious programming on the Mac came later.

Financial

I was very well paid. The people involved in the actual investment management business were very very well paid. The traders were very very very well paid. The typical trader's deal was: We let you use our infrastructure (fancy phone system, fancy ticker and financial news screen, NASDAC trading system to actually make the trades), we give you access to our capital to work with (millions), we give you our backing (so the other side will trade with you), and you keep 45% to 50% of the net profit. They were supposed to stand 45% to 50% of the losses, but it was all cumulative. I don't think the firm could actually extract millions from a net looser, but it sure paid millions to the net winners. Plus year-end bonus. A good description of this culture at this time is the book *Liar's Poker* by Michael Lewis.

Working in the financial industry is like working in a place where millions of dollars are always flowing through a network of pipes. There were always little drips from the pipes. Even the condensation on the outside of the pipes was enough to keep us all well off. My bonus was very much less than millions, but I was very happy with it. I would go around humming "Santa Claus is coming to town" around the beginning of each December. The owner looked like Santa Claus without the beard. Finally you got to go in and visit Santa and come out with your bonus check. I was also given stock options. This happened when the firms was at its zenith. They should have known better than to give me stock options. I am condemned to make my living by dint of hard work, not capital gains. The firm started a slow decline, and I never got anything out of these options.

End of the Age

It seemed as if I worked there for an age. The mid 1980's were nowhere as excessive as the late 2000's in terms of financial wheeling and dealing, but it was an exciting time. I got to watch from the 15th floor as a sky scraper was built not 40 feet away. Eventually I got my own corner office on Montgomery Street. To all external appearances I was this well off capitalist suit. Inside was the same old computer nerd just looking for fun programming assignments.

After the crash in 1987, the business fell off. The firm was sold to some partners who did not want to operate the same way. There was a very long time when nothing seemed to need doing. Although the pay was the same, there was no more bonus.

I decided to become a consultant.

Career Number Three (1988 .. 1993)

Macintosh

During the idle time at the end of my career at the brokerage I was programming the Macintosh. I did several native Mac event driven GUI programs as learning exercises (Fractal viewer, Life simulation). What I decided to concentrate on was to bring business and accounting programming to the Mac.

I wrote a library package that encapsulated the file system. This library supported a common file system interface on the Mac and SUN UNIX. I encapsulated directories, file names, file name paths, and all I/O operations. This was the key to porting all the existing SUN code to the Mac.

First off, I ported all the formatted-screen code. Of course only fixed width fonts would work here. I found a way to bury all of the Mac's GUI event loop in the get-next-key subroutine. That way I could hide the Mac's user-is-in-control way of operating and get back to the good old natural computer-is-in-control way required by the existing code. I liked the Macintosh, but obviously I did not "get it". There was no boss or other co-worker to force me down the right path. But I was having fun.

First Project

My first consulting contract was handed to me by the former owner of the brokerage I had just left. A buddy of his in L.A. operated a very small niche stock brokerage. He wanted to automate their manual way of matching buy and sell orders.

I flew down to L.A. to meet former owner, and we drove over to his buddy's office. He described what they did, and asked me did I want to automate it? I said sure, and we began to discuss price. It was soon apparent that the former owner and his buddy had already kicked around the numbers. The number they were talking about was not huge, but was enough to carry me for a few months. I figured that I could do the work in a few months, so we shook on it and I flew back and started work.

I told the guy in L.A. to order a SUN workstation and have it delivered to my home in Sonoma County. He was to order a second SUN later just prior to the system going live so he would have 100% redundancy. He understood the logic of this, and agreed.

Meanwhile I designed and implemented the system on the Mac. A big part of this was the conversion of the ISAM database I had written many years ago to 'C'. There were a handful of screens, and a few reports. I got it all working on the Mac prior to the SUN arriving at my house.

I started doing all design and development in an incremental manner. I wanted a working program from day one. I would write quite elaborate low level stubs in order to get a working program. As the design of interfaces changed, I would take the trouble to re-work all existing programs. All programs were continually alive and working. Functionality never decreased, only increased. It was OK to merge in new functionality by means of a temporary interface module which would be removed a week later.

I called this the 'pearl' method, because many thin layers were added and polished on top of each other. It got so I hated the idea of writing more than a day's worth of code without being able to make it run.

One major benefit of this way of working was that the design was tested in actual use very early on. Another benefit was that bugs were isolated to some small set of changes. It worked yesterday, but not today. What have I changed?

I divided these early programs into 'applications' and 'placentas'. Later I heard the word 'scaffold' used in a way similar to my 'placenta'. The meaning is slightly different. To me, a scaffold is a static test program that serves to test only a limited part of a system. A placenta evolves with the growing system, and enables testing of the entire system. Indeed, sometimes it is as fully functional as the entire application (albeit with a simple user interface).

One added benefit of the pseudo object-oriented style of programming was that it made creating these test programs easier. This was primarily because the interfaces to the 'objects' was simplified, and designed to work with minimal side effects on the environment.

I started being able to re-use these test programs. The simple user interface code was generic and could be used to test any type of modules. The tests themselves often were similar. As an example, the test rig I set up to exercise the in-memory vector code could be used with little change to test the ISAM data base code.

When the SUN came, I transferred all programs from the Mac over to the SUN, and started testing. I was able to use the Mac as a dumb terminal to provide a second simultaneous user for testing concurrent operation. This all went smoothly, and I was ready to install.

I shipped the SUN down to L.A. and drove down there for several days of install and user training. It turned out that my customer was the husband of a very famous movie star. Her famous films were of the 50's and 60's. He insisted that I stay with them in their Beverly Hills house. They were both very gracious people. I got a home cooked meal and listened to lots of Hollywood gossip and discussed all the current movies.

The install and training went OK. Everything worked as I designed it, but not everything was as the user wanted it. Some of the shortcomings were due to gaps in my understanding, and some were due to the customer's changing requirements. He could see improvements that would greatly simplify the usage of the system. Some of the needed changes were small, one was rather large.

We were able to discuss all of this with good will. Although there was only the most rudimentary written design documentation, he was able to see that some of the "shortcomings" were indeed changes in what he asked for. I agreed that some of the shortcomings were indeed my error. We agreed on the changes and some additional money for me. I guess he was able to see that it would really work and do what he needed, and did not mind spending more. Another factor probably was that the money involved was "chump change" from his perspective.

I made the changes in a few weeks, and he was happy. The system supported four or so terminals in what was essentially an inventory tracking system. It was in use every day and was the heart of his business. I hardly ever heard from him. My goal of "no trouble calls" worked. After it was all over, I calculated that I worked at an hourly rate of $5.00 an hour. I counted it a big success because it worked and was heavily used.

A year later, I got a contract to add a major enhancement to this system. I made a somewhat better hourly rate on this. Then, eight years later I got a call about upgrading. The user wanted to get new SUN machines to replace the old ones. The new machines used Solaris, which was a change from the original SUN OS used on the original work. The 'C' compiler had also changed from old style K&R to so called ANSI-C. This involved function prototypes. A lot of grunge work, and the needed re-testing. I did not want to do this. I was then working full time for a large major corporation.

I told him I was very busy, and could not do the work, but would support and advise any consultant he got to do it. Two weeks later he called back and asked me to just name my price to do the work. I named what I thought was an absurd price. He said, "Done". Once again, I did the work at home, then took two days off work to go over to L.A. and install the new system. He gave me an extra 25% bonus, so I would keep supporting it.

Other Projects

After this project, I worked intermittently on several projects off and on.

The other programmers in the old payroll operation had also left that company to pursue the goal of running business programs on Data General Equipment. They hired me to do the occasional COBOL job. They wanted me to do more, but I saw no future in COBOL on Data General equipment. The brokerage company also needed occasional help with the programs I had written when I was there.

The main thing I was working on was a small accounting system for the Mac. This was a General Ledger with many reports suitable for a small business or household use. It was a different design from what I had done at the brokerage, but was based on the same low level "classes". It had that 80x25 formatted screen look and feel.

The Future of programming

I read the Mac magazines and noticed that the reviews all gave great weight to look and feel as well as Mac like operation. By comparison my application looked like a throwback to mainframe timeshare applications. The meteor had hit and the climate was changing. A bunch of small new style programs were running about, and older ways of doing interactive programming were feeling a chill in the air.

In my mind it was frivolous. The new style used up 90% of the memory and CPU for flash and sizzle. The older character based formatted screen techniques were so very efficient in terms of memory and CPU use. This was not about functionality. I could do pop-ups to select from a list, completion of partially filled in fields, and all the rest of it. With function keys, the user had some sort of control, but the data entry clerks I knew (and I had known many over the years) all valued efficient key sequences, and being led by the computer while filling in a form. Moving the hand over to the mouse was awkward and a waste of time.

Back in 1978 we would discuss the future of programming. I spoke of an analogy to the automobile industry. We were in the "model T" era. At some point the technologists would lose control to bean counters and fashion. It was just amusing B.S. type talking on my part. I had an IMSAI 8080 microcomputer and did not see any potential for changing the current technologist driven model. If anything, there was a premium on clever programming to get anything useful out of an eight bit CPU with 16 KB RAM.

When I worked for the broker in 1983, we went on a field trip to SUN microsystems. Some of the guys in the office had invested in SUN, and we got a tour of the new office as they were moving. Fat, yellow Ethernet cable all over the floor, empty rooms. But I saw a 3" hard drive with the capacity of our rack mounted unit that they were going to put into a desktop workstation. I was already impressed with SUN equipment. It was a quantum leap from the DG stuff I was used to. Here was a 32 bit processor and 8MB of RAM in a small rack, soon to be in a desktop unit. This was equivalent to the IBM 360 of my undergrad days.

I was amazed, and thought I understood how to use all of that power. When NEWS (SUN's GUI style bitmapped graphics stuff) came out I thought this was just a gimmick. NEWS made the SUN run dog slow. It crashed all the time. What an expensive waste. Let's not even start discussing the waste inherent in color displays.

The Mac brought a 32 bit 2 MB RAM unit to the desk in my own home, but it was saddled with this enervating OS. Reading the Mac magazines, you could clearly see the fashion reporting. Ratings on visual effects. "New" looks. You could start to actually tell that a given program had the "old" look.

What was a bull session analogy about the auto industry back in 1978 was now coming true in front of my eyes. The Mac was like smoothly bent, brightly colored metal. Stylists had been involved in the OS. I admired the new, mouse driven GUI style, and I saw the programming challenge in writing such code. Later, I even made a living writing MS-Windows GUI's. But, I never respected it the way I respected systems or business programming.

My failure to understand and embrace these changes was a major mistake.

Partnership (1990 .. 1992)

I heard from my former boss at the Gold trader's operation. While I was working for the broker, he had quit and become a consultant. He was more outgoing than I was, and had made many contacts in the financial community over those years. He was making a living writing small IBM PC applications using Borland's Turbo Pascal.

My friend and another friend of his asked me if I wanted to form a partnership to do consulting to the financial industry. I said "yes". Our new partnership rented a one room office in Sonoma County. I bought a TRS-80 with 640KB RAM and 20MB disk and Turbo Pascal. We were off and running.

The three of us quickly established a very collaborative working relationship. This was similar to the way I worked at the insurance rating company. We had lengthy discussions on design and trends in the industry. I was fortunate and did not know it. This was to be the last time in my career I was able to be part of this good of a working relationship.

A large part of the business was writing specialized report programs for a popular IBM PC based portfolio accounting system. We had figured out the database formats, and wrote Pascal programs to create specialty reports based on the data entered by the standard input programs. We also created supplemental data files with our own input programs. These custom reports saved so much work in certain situations that we could make a living creating them.

I wrote a Mac based program that converted MS-Word on the Mac "doc" files to plain text ASCII files. I preserved as much of the formatting and spacing as I could. These text files were then posted to primitive BBS systems. (I wrote away to Microsoft for the "doc" file format specification and they actually sent it to me.) We also learned about Novell network installation. We configured and set up small computer networks for small investment advisors.

All of our contracts were for roughly $10,000 dollars, payable after delivery of the product. We could not get a bigger contract without involving more people at our customer's office. That would mean time consuming proposal writing with no guarantee that we would get the business. All of our sales were informal discussions between my partners and one other person at the customer's office. The $10,000 seemed to be the typical limit to which one person could commit. I soon realized that we were not doing what serious businessman should be doing. We made no effort to do the proposal writing needed to go after larger contracts. We made little effort to seek out and sell to strangers. Many of our customers wanted support for their office networks. We did this only grudgingly. Fact is, two of us had no love for the financial industry, and we wanted to program for the love of it.

Race Cars

My friend from Southern California had an interest in car racing. He had built and driven a small Bonneville race car in his younger days. He held a land speed record for a class of small car and engine. He had many buddies who did Bonneville and Drag racing as a hobby. He wanted to develop a small on-board performance monitor for these types of race cars. We may even have discussed this prior to forming the partnership.

We found a supplier of Z-80 based embedded systems. My partner designed the signal conditioning circuits. I did the programming. The other partner worked the old business to bring in $$$. We developed a small (10" x 6" x 3") unit that could measure crank shaft RPM, Drive shaft RPM, Oil pressure, and various temperatures. It had a two-line LCD display, and a 12-key pad on the front. The data was polled from the sensors and stored on-board. After the race, you attached a small Epson compatible printer, and the unit would print out graphs, or dump the data in Lotus-123 format.

It worked! You could alter the data polling to accommodate an 8 second drag race, or a 4 minute Bonneville run. Our motto was "Save just one engine from burning up, and you have paid for the unit". My partner could read the graphs like a Mayo Clinic specialist could read X-rays. We saved many an engine. We enabled performance tuning that resulted in observable gains in speed.

We could sell these units as long as my partner consulted on the installation. (For free, of course). We needed design feedback, so this made sense. Every other customer said "Yep, I'll buy it if it can do X". So we would make it do "X". This was market research. But, the specifications never seemed to converge. In any case we sold enough to make a living. It was a smaller living than the financial reporting, but oh so much more fun.

The culmination of this was when the unit was put into a stock car that was doing speed trials at Bonneville Salt Flats. The data from the unit was valuable and used to tune the engine to the point where it performed much better than it had ever done. There is a video of this car's final run where it went so fast, it literally took off. It flew 5 feet above the ground, twisted in the air, then hit the ground and rolled for a long time till it stopped. No one was hurt, and the data logger was still functioning.

Partnership change

Our third partner was not having as much fun. He wanted out. He could make a living doing the financial reporting. It was obvious that we were not going to all become rich with the race car computer any time soon. There were no hard feelings. We bought him out. It was now a two man partnership, my friend and me. We kept the same office and stopped even pretending to do financial programming.

We wanted to make a much smaller unit based on the Intel 8051. This was an 8 bit processor optimized for embedded systems. We found a supplier that packaged it with 32KB RAM in an enclosure that looked like an old fashioned null-modem. It had a D25 connector at each end. The pins were all assigned to analog, digital signals and power. Interfacing was easy, just buy a regular D25 connector, solder up the right wires and away you go. This time there were no controls on the unit. You connected to the COM1: port of a PC and ran a special program.

Again I did all programming. This involved the PC based control program as well as the embedded system. All programming was in 8051 assembly language. There was no OS, so that was part of the work. We developed and sold a handful of programs on this platform. It was the most fun I ever had in my career.

First off we re-implemented the race car performance logger. We sold these, and made requested enhancements. We adapted it to monitor small handheld motors like weed whackers or leaf blowers. We thought the data on the actual use of these small motors would be of interest. The kind of data collected (RPM, temperature) allowed accurate estimates of the amount of actual use each unit got, and the pollution actually produced. It turns out that owners of large numbers of these units (like grounds keepers) did not care. The EPA cared, but we did not want to deal with the government.

Fork in the Road

The second application was very different. We got a customer who was a retired servo motor engineer. He had a contract with a company in Germany to control a post-press processor. This is a unit that goes on the end of a large newspaper or magazine press. It does things like put stickers onto each page. The problem is to keep this unit in sync with the pages as they go by. It is not connected with the press controls, so must optically scan the page looking for some sort of mark on each. It gets inputs from the servomotors, and optical sensors. The operator input is an angular setting for how far down the page to put the sticker. The output is a PID (Proportional, Integral, and Derivative) feedback control signal to a servo motor.

This project worked because the customer knew exactly what he wanted. No way were we going to get a newspaper press in our office, so the customer helped us design a test rig that had the same sort of inputs. It was a saw blade with markings on it run by a servomotor. The optical sensor watching it was put on a stack of magazines. We would spin the saw blade at 120 to 200 RPM and watch the angle at which the marks were seen by the sensor. Placing weights (like a penny) onto the top of the sensor would very slightly change its displacement (compress the magazines more or less) and change this angle. We would see the output signal on the O-scope. This was just at the limits of the processing power of the 8051. I needed to re-design and code the interrupt service four times before I got the needed performance. My partner designed the interface board for input signal filtering, and output control signals. We also had a small keypad and LCD display for operator setup.

After the last performance enhancement, I still had a problem with the timing. The angle calculated had a random jitter of a fraction of a degree. I triple checked the performance of the interrupt and calculation routines using the O-scope to convince myself that this randomness was not an artifact of my programming. I finally confessed to the customer that the processing was not within specifications, would result in poor output signals and I had no idea why.

The customer grinned, and came back next day with a different optical sensor. The old one was cheap, and used an LED. This new one was expensive, and used a bright incandescent lamp. He explained that LED light was pulsed, based on the AC current frequency. The randomness I was seeing was due to the LED rapidly switching on and off. After the incandescent lamp was installed, my code calculated exact angles with no jitter. Like I said, the customer knew his stuff. He was impressed I was able to detect this jitter, and impressed that I had confessed to it. The customer took the units we built to Germany, and successfully installed them. I think of this project as the high point of my career as a solo designer and implementer of software. However, the money was not great.

The customer was retired, but he held several patents for servomotor control, and knew many high up people in companies that made them. He took me to lunch, and said he could get me a good job down in Silicon Valley. It was too far to commute, and I was still operating on the good place to live has priority over job theory. But another theory is work with super competent people who know more than you do. After some thought, I declined the offer. In retrospect, this was a major fork in the road for my career. I do not know if I regret this decision or not.

The third project was to control a chip inspection machine. The guy across the hall was a mechanical engineer. On contract he designed a machine to inspect the visual markings on chips made by a small IC manufacturer. There were three asynchronous stages to this operation, and the job was challenging. This worked well, and went into production. If this guy across the hall expanded, we would have no doubt gotten more contracts, as it was, this job just tided us through a few months.

The last job was to experiment with the brake controls of wind turbines. Apparently, the brake system just locked on and stopped them as quickly as possible. Cracks were developing in the blades due to this stress. The company wanted to experiment with pumping the brakes, and stopping more slowly.

This involved tapping into the existing control system and overriding the brake servo output line. They had a simulator we were able to use for our debug. After we got it working, time to go to the wind farm on Altamont Pass east of San Francisco. It worked as designed, the windmills stopped more slowly, with less stress on the blades. But we noticed that pumping the brakes quickly depleted the hydraulic pressure. During one trial, we almost ran out of pressure before the blades stopped.

Hobbies

A self-employed man has no hobbies. Or, in my case you could say that the entire partnership was a hobby, and I had no serious job.

Partnership Divorce

The money kept rolling in, but at a much-reduced rate. The recession in the early 1990s hit California's aerospace industry hard. Guess where all these race car hobbyists were employed? They owned machine shops that catered to the aerospace industry. We diversified by capitalizing on our experience on the 8051 platform. The most fun programming I ever had came from these diverse projects. The money still came in. It was cruel. If there was no money at all, we could have realized we needed to quit. There was money, but just not quite enough to live on.

A year previously, I had busted my IRA accumulated during the fat brokerage years. Paid the 10% penalty. Now that was gone. I knew in my heart we were not serious businessmen, and so never even considered a second mortgage on the house, whose value was greatly inflated by the California real estate boom. It was time to go off on my own.

A business partnership has many similarities to a marriage. There are common finances, so you need to trust your partner totally. Breaking a partnership requires dividing the assets. If one side wants to keep going, then he must buy the other out (or the other partner must walk away with nothing). It was a very emotional decision. I had known my partner for fifteen years. It was done, and I was on my own again in a recession.

Interlude (1993)

I was essentially un-employed. I made a resume, and got many interviews, but no job. In one case they gave me a programming test which I knew I aced. It had a few questions from the old punch card days that I answered, but I doubt anyone younger could have. No go. No good reason. Could it be the gray in my hair?

I tried body shops, where they got you contracts and took 50% of the money. No dice. I tried head-hunters. I knew those guys got 50% of your first year's salary as their fee. They were all buzzword oriented. Did you know CICS? RPG? How many years' experience on the XYZ ICE? I passed few of the buzzword tests, and my assurances that I could pick up and be effective doing anything were met with shrugs. In one situation, I hit it off well in an interview I got through sending my resume directly to the company. Until they heard about my relationship with the headhunter. Apparently they would have had to pay him, even though he had not made the introduction. Or so they said.

This was a very depressing time. I was not able to get a job on my terms. I knew that my age had a lot to do with my failure during interviews. The guy interviewing me was much younger. I think my experience level came through the interview, but the guy probably thought of the possible attitude problems, or lack of energy in an older guy. They were probably right, I would have become frustrated working for them, and become a pain in the ass. I just didn't have it in me to put on a smile, shoe shine, and go cold calling. I would need to act confident, say "piece of cake" and be willing to commute all over the bay area.

During this time I set about to learn Windows GUI programming. I bought Petzold's book. I had an Intel 486 with 8MB RAM and a color monitor from the partnership. Using Borland's C++ compiler and OWL GUI package, I started in. I did not realize it at the time, but GUI programming is perhaps the best way to learn object oriented programming and C++. Borland's OWL package was well thought out. The GUI objects form a natural set of inheritance trees. The document/view and facade models have a natural use in this realm.

Combined with my prior experience with "classes" and "objects" in the 'C' language, the practical use of inheritance in OWL gave me solid 'C++' mastery. My work on the Macintosh gave me an excellent education on GUI programming in general. I read many books on C++ at the time, but by far the best of them (for an experienced programmer) is B. Stroustrup's *The C++ Programming Language, 2nd ed.* I think that a major factor in C++ catching on so well is Stroustrup's excellent clarity in writing. Another excellent book is Stroustrup's *The Design and Evolution of C++*.

Small Company

I finally got a juicy contract with a local small software company. This company did simple advertising type applications that ran in kiosks using a touch screen. They displayed flashy graphics and had a simple user interface. They wanted to branch out into more complex business applications. My past experience was just what they were looking for. They wanted me to do a medium sized investment tracking application for their customer on the East coast.

I did the work using my existing character based PC library. When it came time to present the results to the customer on the East coast, the local company representative was ill, so I flew to the East coast solo for the customer demo. The customer loved the application, and signed off. I flew back and only then did anyone from the local company see it. When they saw my two color 80x24 fixed width screen formats they were appalled. Their existing applications hid behind an elaborate visual presentation. But they took the client's money. They were convinced I knew my business programming stuff and offered me a job.

I learned an interesting technique in my brief stay there. One of the artists explained that if you had a limited color palette, you needed to use colors in light dark pairs. That is, each color you were using needed to have both a lighter and a darker shade. Then you could create shading and shadows even though there was only a limited color range. The results were impressive. I used this idea later in my needlepoint designs.

Big Company

Prior to this job, while I was still un-employed, an old friend from my Burroughs days came to visit. He was currently working at one of the plants of a very large company in a small state in the Pacific Northwest. He said his team really needed a new guy, and I gave him my resume.

Large companies move slowly, but they finally flew me over for an interview. My master's degree was a big plus. This was the first time since I got the degree 20 years ago that it mattered in any way.

They wanted a GUI programmer. I took a floppy with my latest hobby horse. The interview was intensive. One guy asked me to write code to insert a node into an ordered singly linked list. Normally, I would have been sunk because of my inability to think on my feet accurately, or fast. I had often written such code 15 years ago, but by some amazing stroke of luck, I had written just that very code in the prior month. This effort came back to mind, and I did OK. Another interviewer asked to see my hobby horse, and was amused with it. Another interviewer wanted to know why I did not mortgage my house to keep the partnership going.

The family was willing. This new town was also a very good place to live and raise a family. After months of un-employment, I had truly psyched myself to put aside my aversion to large companies. We could take a lot of cash money out of our California house, and live like kings in this new state.

No offer. My friend called to say that there was an edict from on high freezing all hiring. Oh well. Meanwhile, I had the job at the small advertising company. After being there one month, I finally got a call from a manager at the large out-of-state company to whom I had never spoken. Did I want a job? I gave notice at the small company, and was at my desk in the big company within two weeks. This was early in the year, so the family stayed back in California to sell the house and finish out the school year.

In retrospect, it is interesting how my old negative attitude about working for a large corporation was suppressed. I was down to zero savings, I had a wife and two kids, I had no health insurance, I had no retirement plan, I was way over 40 years old, which made it very difficult to change jobs. Without being aware of any contradictions, my attitude at the beginning was: This is going to work out well. There will be no problems. And it was true. At first

Career Number Four (1994 .. 2002)

Phase I - GUI Guru (1994 .. 1995)

My job was to take over lead development of a GUI application used to configure and manage a new RAID disk array device the company was developing. I plunged into the task with lots of enthusiasm. The current design called for new windows to be created for each new task. The user soon faced a cluttered, overlapping mess. I wanted a tabbed dialog sort of application. Tabbed dialogs were then new, and the coming fashion. I argued with my co-developer, with marketing, and other team mates. I was diplomatic and persistent and got this changed. This started me off on the right foot.

I was seen as a MS-Windows and GUI expert. This was an exotic specialty, as the rest of the lab was heavily into UNIX. The irony ! I wanted in the worst way to join the UNIX types doing the embedded firmware for the new device, but here I was, stuck in the role of dilettante fashion conscious GUI programmer. I played the role seriously, and did not talk about my background. At one point there was a heated discussion in my cube on shades of blue versus gray. Later on, people started ribbing me about this. Many had overheard, and found it amusing that anyone could take such a thing so seriously.

I was surprised that everyone in this company called themselves "engineer". My title was "software engineer". I never thought of what I did as "engineering". "Skilled trade", "artisan", "craftsman" were more like it. Sometimes, my ego would swell and I thought of myself as "artist" (as in a writer of novels). Never engineer. Engineers dealt in a very systematic way with real objects. Steam tables, tensile strengths, inductance, resistance were some of the things engineers dealt with.

There were by now time honored best practices in the realm of software. Things like "structured programming", "waterfall model", "spiral model", "object oriented programming". The trouble was, few of these practices were followed. They were too slow and too expensive for practical work. Besides, these "best practices" kept changing. Software was too immature for "engineering". Apprentice, Journeyman, Master was more like it for the art of programming. I actually had a hard time calling myself an engineer. I thought my old friends from college would think I was pretentious. I have no trouble with this now. Some words become de-valued over time. Software still has a long way to go before becoming "engineering". Look for the first successful lawsuit against a programmer for engineering malfeasance.

The architecture, established long before I got there, was client/server. The server communicated directly with the device, and used LAN networking to communicate with the GUI client. Both sides were in C++. At first, the only client would be the GUI running on 16 bit MS-Windows. There were two of us working on the client, and the rest of the team was on the server.

I wanted to understand the entire system, so I went to a meeting of the server group. I had my first rude shock. My presence there was challenged. The attitude was: We have defined an interface, just read the document. Although I was allowed to stay, it was clear that comments or questions would be most un-welcome.

I needed the feedback loop of a functional system in order to do development and design. There was no way I was going to design and code as much code as a GUI takes without being able to do it in an incremental way. That required a working server, which in turn required a working device. These did not exist, so I wrote a fairly elaborate "fake" of the client/server interface backed by a simple state machine to model the device. To make this work, I would ask people over in the firmware team what the sequence of responses to various configuration commands would be. This way I could develop real GUI code, and show demos of real functionality. To my amazement, none of the other engineers thought this "fake" was a good idea. Most thought I was wasting time, some thought I was grandstanding because the demo got wide visibility.

The GUI development lead to weekly user interface meetings with marketing and formal one way mirror user interface trials. I enjoyed all of these discussions, and the chore of creating prototypes of the screens. A few times, the design called for functionality that was not in the client/server interface. Try as I might to be low key, diplomatic, and professional, this was taken badly by the server team. They spoke of end-runs, over stepping bounds. When I spoke with firmware developers to try and see what functionality was possible, I was told by my team members to never speak with those guys, and go through one of the server team members.

This did not frustrate me as much as I thought it would. I developed relationships with many reasonable people. By its nature, the GUI was very visible outside the project. I had many discussions with people outside the group. Some team members became envious of my visibility, and retaliated by not inviting me to meetings to discuss changes to functionality in the client/server interface. What a petty mess.

The project managers, or first level bosses were somewhat aware of what was going on, but were not too concerned. The managers had no technical role. They went to meetings with other bosses, and communicated edicts to the troops in weekly meetings. Managers were specifically and actively excluded from technical discussions.

I found this odd. I looked for how the technical work was organized, and found no clear cut official mechanism. Some people had a lot of technical influence, but you were always free to skip meetings, and do things your own way. Everyone was presumed fully competent to do any task they were given. If you wanted to get help, you could find a sympathetic buddy with patience and time to spare. Or you could blunder on, and others would work around your shortcomings.

Management did not seem to involve itself in any of this sort of thing. Shouldn't an R&D lab actively cultivate and grow competence? Indeed, I was hired because the guy responsible for the GUI client could not get along with the server people. The result was that the interface had no input from the client side, and the work was headed for failure. The technical and personal issues he raised were not addressed by management, instead he was pushed aside, and I was hired.

I paid close attention to the "real" functionality in the firmware, and kept my "fake" functionality compatible. The switch from "fake" to "real" was painless. On the day that we got the first live connection between the GUI and a prototype of the device, they canceled the GUI project.

My first Re-Org

It seems that the plan to market the device to consumers in Comp USA type stores was wrong. A quote from one of the meetings announcing the change: "It is really a lifestyle choice; buy one of our units, or a backyard swimming pool". Our new device was really better suited to be connected to large UNIX workstations or servers. What was really wanted was a traditional UNIX command line interface to the device.

Until now, I had been operating in my old mode of application development. I was trying to please my customers, whom I thought were the marketing department and the usability lab. I was concentrating on the details of design and implementation. The trouble I had with some un-helpful, secretive people proved to be surmountable. Surely the marketing department of a huge international company knew what it was doing. I took my head out of the sand and became aware of what most of the others knew all along. Another division of the company in another state was developing devices similar to ours for attachment to WinTel boxes. That other division was feuding with ours. Where our marketing folks got their info, I don't know. This other division had their own marketing people; apparently they arrived at different conclusions.

Time for my first re-org. A re-org is when management three or so levels up changes. It takes a long time for the practical consequences of this to be felt. Sometimes managers lower down would then be changed. This took a while. Sometimes general edicts would be handed down from on high, but no immediate action could be taken, because no one lower down seemed to have authority (or perhaps the guts) to do anything for a month or so. I saw ten or so of these re-orgs during my eighteen years there. Meanwhile, nothing much to do. I pinned the Dilbert cartoon about Wally's "In-cube sabbatical" on my cube wall.

The work environment at my level in this firm was completely different from a technical person interacting with a business owner. Or even a technical person interacting with a marketing department. I was interacting with a boss. My boss had a boss. My boss' boss had a boss. We were still five layers from a business owner. The best model I could come up with was a Feudal model. I owed fealty to my boss, my boss owed me protection. My boss' goals became my goals. If my boss could advance, then so could I. To step outside of this simple model required a thorough understanding of Machiavelli. I had read and admired that book, but I knew I could never play those games. Now, what mattered was: Was my liege lord in favor at the Duke's court? Was our Duchy going places? How liberal would my lord be with patronage? Is the King powerful enough to make all the Dukes work to a common purpose? Were these wars just local land grabs, or was there a real national interest at stake?

I made a very conscious decision to play the role of trusted technical advisor to my current boss. I would master all relevant technical issues, and be totally open and candid with my boss about all technical issues. I hoped that my boss would value this. For this to work, the boss must be willing to have open detailed discussions about technical issues. I was to find out that not all were. I was to find that my particular Duchy was caught up in a seemingly endless series of "war of the roses". The kingdom kept changing hands, and the Duke himself was executed and replaced with the new king's favorite several times. This is not a good environment for undertaking anything that takes longer than a year to complete.

Demos

Finally, the manager two levels up and one over wanted to get the GUI completed. He wanted to use it as a demo tool. It showed the unique capabilities of the new device in a very effective way. But the manager three levels up must absolutely NOT know about this. So I finished work on the GUI. It was taken to UNIX trade shows where it was connected to an UNIX based server and showed off the capabilities of the new device well.

The board of directors was coming to town. The new device was to be demonstrated. The firmware folks put together a cart with all of the equipment, and included a PC running the GUI for the demo. The device itself was just a box. The only thing to see was the GUI's representation of what was going on inside the box. Unfortunately, the person doing the demo was that manager three levels up. He pitched a fit. He was not interested in learning anything about a GUI. So a glass teletype running the command line was substituted. The demo was just all talk. Absolutely nothing to see.

I asked the manager for whom I had finished the GUI (who was in charge of the firmware) for a transfer to firmware. Nope. I was seen as a dilettante who argued about shades of blue. Others from my team were transferred over. I transferred to the firmware section of a different division based at the same site that made a different sort of product.

Phase II - Firmware Engineer (1996 .. 1997)

This was just like changing to a different company. I had to interview. Did I understand about multi-threaded programming? Once hired, I had no respect from new peers till I proved it by months of work.

I was hired to maintain a file system that could access an optional disk drive installed in the device. I studied up on file systems, but I needn't have bothered. They had purchased an MS-DOS FAT based file system from a third party, and adapted it to the homegrown OS.

This device was powered on and off at will by the user. Especially to recover from error conditions. The FAT file system is vulnerable to corruption on power loss. I could get no one else to care. I noticed that they would rather buy new technology from small third parties and adapt rather than grow their own. I wrote a "chkdsk" function that would find and repair corruption. It could not be part of normal boot because it would delay start of operations, so I made it work if some magic key sequence was pressed on boot. It was shipped with the product, but no one really cared. I was never told why my worries about corruption were invalid.

It was OK. There was lots of very cool equipment to learn about. In Circuit Emulators, execution path trace capture. There was a clever UNIX workstation-based application that used every sophisticated feature in UNIX to do a very good simulation of the device. I learned lots of new techniques. I switched to EMACS as my editor. I slowly built up relationships. I was many layers removed from the marketing department, so I mainly talked shop with the people in my department.

The block level interface between the file system and the disk drive was owned by a different group. The guy was 9 or 10 cubicle rows away. He was actively rude. Actively unhelpful. He gave the strong impression I had no right to speak with him. Late in the project he needed me, because bugs would turn up in testing, and it was not immediately clear whose layer was at fault. He would dump some on me, which I would investigate and solve in his layer. I would always deal directly with him when I returned the results, never his manager. I thought I was building bridges.

When the next big re-org came, the functionality I was responsible for was transferred to this guy's group. It was not clear what else there was for me to do. I went down to his group and asked to come over. No direct answer, but two weeks later I found out that they had hired someone from outside the company and had given the job to him.

Back to square one for me. Two years' experience in this area was now worthless. If I had been younger, I might think I was a marginal performer. If someone told me this story of not continuing my job in the new group, I would conclude that probably the story teller was one of those marginally competent hard-to-get-along-with types. In fact, it was likely due to a common close-knit religion among the other team's members. It is no fun to be discriminated against.

It's every man for themselves in a re-org. My boss was transferring to a different division, so I had no patron. I wound up in a new group with a boss devoted to old friends, and a detailed devotion to the formal process. Part of the job interview was to assess how much I knew about the formal process of developing software. Notions like "Requirements document", "External Reference Specification", "Design Review", "Code Review", "Functionality Complete", "Regression Test", "Code Complete", "Manufacturing Release". I had a very good working understanding of all of this, but did not know any of these terms. I think I just barely passed this portion of the interview. Or perhaps I flunked. But it did not really matter, because it was all just talk.

What really happened was the requirements were for "all of the above". There was never enough time to write a definitive external reference, so the best efforts first draft changed from day to day. Functionality complete was a date on a calendar that meant time was running out. Code complete meant that you had to be extra careful about the changes you made after that date. The notion of running the complete test suite after the LAST code change was abandoned.

People talked about the correct procedures as if talking about a bygone golden age. I really do not know to what extent they were ever really practiced. Although they result in a high-quality product, they are slow, and expensive. For all of the talk about "teamwork", what was valued and rewarded was extreme individual effort to make it happen. One hero achieved that status by single handedly saving a late project, then being hospitalized for exhaustion. An absolute must-read on the subject of managing software development is *The Mythical Man-Month, Anniversary Edition*, by Frederick P. Brooks, Jr. In my experience, all of the discussion in this book is dead on. Everyone I have ever talked to agrees. No management team ever follows its advice.

I still thought there was hope for a rewarding technical assignment at this big company, so I transferred back to the division I had left two years ago. I thought back to what I had been able to accomplish in two years time at the Insurance rating company, or the investment advisor/ broker and felt very frustrated.

Learnings

After working in this big company for a number of years, the banalities that "Big projects need many people to do the work.", "In a big group of people, most will be average.", and "In a big group of people, some will be hard to get along with." hit home. The most important problem to solve in a big project is how to organize, and motivate the people. In a large enough group of people, some level of technical competence can be taken for granted, and the purely technical problems can be assumed to be solvable. The first line manager becomes the most important job. This is also the toughest job.

I think of this as the "second lieutenant" job. This person is under pressure from the higher officers who may or may not make reasonable demands. This person is also under pressure from the people in his charge doing the technical work, who may make reasonable or un-reasonable demands. Occasions arise where loyalty to the management (of which he is a member) requires less than total candor when motivating his troops. If the front-line manager has a difficult situation because of the nature of his charges, and yet succeeds, the higher-level bosses may never know. Unlike a technical person, a major tool for his success on the job is the performance of other people.

The problem of organizing large numbers of people is as old as civilization, and there are many recorded success stories. There are many recorded failures. Reading history did not comfort me in this regard. Military history shows that even with their lives on the line, management can still indulge in petty in-fighting, and because of that, make ultimately stupid decisions that lead to general destruction. In a fat company, where total failure means a severance package, where is the feedback loop that will eventually insure success?

Given all of these uncertainties, the only stable thing I can see is personal trust between two individuals. This trust grows out of a long term relationship. I never fault a new high level manager for trying any and all means to bring trusted people into responsible positions; it is the only way they have to influence their own chances for success.

This trust can more easily be developed down the management chain. You have more opportunities to observe the people that work for you, and see who to trust. You can then direct work assignments to optimize your chances of success. Developing trust up the management chain is much more difficult. The only way I know requires at least a year of solid performance and support for your boss, and it only works if your boss is even willing to develop trust in the first place.

All of these observations are consistent with Feudalism. The predicted result is: there can be some glorious successes, or some 30 years of constant war. Overall progress is possible but very slow. Some general conclusions I drew are:

- In a small company look for the cool technical problem, in a large company look for the cool boss or organization.

- In a large company there is a tension between loyalty to your boss and your own success. On the one hand, loyalty may result in trust from above, and trust from above can lead to advancement. On the other hand, sticking around in a losing organization results in limited advancement. You cannot change the fate of a losing organization.

- You cannot advance while telecommuting, or working from home. Developing trusting relationships over a long distance takes a long time.

- Rapid creative technical collaboration requires so much bandwidth and respect among those involved, that the maximum distance between the individuals of the group can be at most about 100 feet. Thus, cross site development must be done at a high technical level (e.g., SCSI interface) or else a slow pace must be tolerated.

- It is OK to enjoy the perks of position. Often that is the only reward there is.

For me, all of this was depressing. I am not able to enjoy any "perks", and could never think that the paycheck was all I needed from a job. I could never tell my boss anything other than the truth as I saw it. If by doing that, my boss became uncomfortable, then I lost their trust. I always was emotionally involved in the success of the project I was on. I could never put on blinders, and just concentrate on the pure technical issue. I needed to believe that the technical problem I was working on was contributing to the overall success of the project.

Phase III Software Technical Lead (1998 .. 2001)

While I was gone, this division had undergone another Re-org. They now had more money, and a large commitment to the second generation of the product. All of the good will and respect I had built up there instantly returned to me when I came back. I was pleasantly surprised by this.

I started off maintaining the old server code. Soon, a new project manager was hired and the team split. The new manager was given responsibility for adapting the code to the new second generation device. This new manager was one of my old co-workers from my first year there.

He had a similar background to mine (small companies), had been hired the same time I had, and had also transferred out to a different division when I did. Now we were both back. I had gotten along with him well three years ago, now he was my boss.

Soon after this, there was another re-org in the way in which device management software was to be written. It would now be architected at a higher level in the company. Although the leadership for this effort was at a different site in a different state, our device was chosen to be the first practical example.

The new system was to be implemented in Java. Although there was a nominal technical lead in our section, my boss pushed me forward. He got me invited to planning and architectural meetings. I hit it off well with the lead designers of the higher-level system. We had similar backgrounds and philosophy in program design. I brought lots of practical experience managing this type of device that others did not have. I was invited back to all meetings, and started traveling. The nominal technical lead of our group was sometimes invited, and sometimes not. My efforts to collaborate with this person were un-successful. This nominal technical lead had been hired right out of college at the same time I was hired. So they got the job of technical lead after four years work experience.

We had few conversations. They always went badly from my perspective. I could seldom get the conversation down to specifics. They kept the discussion in the realm of buzzwords and generalities. They terminated one discussion by saying they had a headache. I was made to feel that I was too stupid for discussions at a high enough level. However, I had a good idea of what technical collaboration was all about, and had done it very successfully in the past. I also communicated well with the tech lead of the project at the other site, so I just dealt with him.

My boss asked me if I wanted a formal promotion to tech lead. I was already doing the work, but knew that the formal job required many management meetings, slide ware, and presentations. I said "No". He put on the hard sell. I resisted. Finally, he said it was ready to go, what was my final decision? I agonized over this. I wanted to support my boss as well as he supported me. I finally told him "No" again. I could do the job and get the influence I needed through my interactions with the tech leads in the higher-level project.

In our lab, formal technical leads were supposed to operate on a higher plane. There was a chart that showed how many years in the future a technical lead was supposed to be operating based on job title. There was a statement that technical leads should not be coding. One tech lead I knew told me he was warned that his performance review would suffer if he did not stop coding so much, and should start working at a more "blue sky" level. I was unhappy with this rule for several reasons.

- First, there was no technical leadership at the actual implementation level. The implementation level was not working so well in my opinion, and needed leadership. It was apparent that leadership on that level was not valued.

- Second, to really operate two years in the future required collaboration with other labs. Our lab was not responsible for a big enough part of what the customer perceived as a "solution". This cooperation among labs planning several years out was not going to be driven from our lab. There was in fact no such serious, full time effort that occupied the tech leads being driven from anywhere.

- Third, the half-life of any coherent multi-site technical strategy was one year. Then a re-org usually brought in new committees and strategies.

Two days later, I was promoted by a manager at the other site. There was no interview or process, it was just done. Those jobs were heavily sought after, and normally there was an interview. I went along with it out of loyalty to my boss. The nominal tech lead in my group told me there was going to be trouble and there would be a lot of resentment. I never encountered any, except for that one individual.

I helped design the details of the Java interface for our device. I sent out a document discussing the tradeoffs of re-writing our stuff in Java, or writing a glue layer to the existing C++ server. I got zero response. So I decided to re-write the server in Java. No one (including me) had ever programmed in Java before. We were working hard and having fun.

Re-org

The re-org gives, and the re-org takes away. This next re-org removed the driving force behind the higher level architecture. We were on our own to do all work locally again. The organization at the other site got a levee of two bosses and 20 engineers from our site. Paralysis while the two and twenty were chosen. My boss elected to go. (All of his protection and support was at the other site anyway). I did not like the look of the new group's work assignments. I elected to stay and see through the device management I had helped design. I had no protection. My new boss was someone new to the division.

The boss two levels up inherited me, but made it clear he had faith and trust in the nominal tech lead. He also made it clear he wanted to hire an old buddy of his as formal tech lead for this Java project. I resigned my tech lead role, and said I would do whatever was needed to help the project. I had no "political" ambitions. I only wanted to do technical work. I had a great deal of de-facto influence prior to the promotion, and figured I would have it after I stepped down. This was indeed true.

The favorite of the big boss left the company after a month. After several weeks of confusion, I was asked to take up the de-facto tech lead role again. So again I had the duties, but not the formal job title. This suited me very well.

The next year was a very busy time. I was heavily engaged in design discussions, Java coaching, and actual implementation. The project was completely local, and I was able to obtain all of the cooperation needed. The team got along well. There was always someone in my cube for a technical discussion, or for advice. I was able to un-officially act as "chief programmer".

I had done no GUI programming since 1995. Now, I learned 'Swing', and did some GUI programming again. Java was actually taking over many OS functions in its quest for OS independence. I admired this, and had hopes this would keep on being developed. I invested heavily in learning the details of Java.

In the middle of this, another re-org resulted in changes to the hardware platform and functionality of the device itself. This rippled down to the device management software we were working on. It had the effect of further delaying release of any new product from our lab, but the product finally did release. The alignment of conditions that gave me so much influence changed. Two bosses up was convinced that the older nominal tech lead had actually done the leadership work (I know because I asked him directly), and that person started becoming active in discussions on how to interface our software with outside groups. I had mixed feelings, I really did not want a politically powerful position, I just wanted technical respect. I had that from my peers if not from management. After all, I had resigned the formal technical lead job. I had no regrets over that move.

As the project wound down, I was pushed to think about my future at the company. I could see what was needed to become a project manager, and thought I could do the job. But as the job was done in my lab, I knew I would hate it. I could continue being a technical lead for a large implementation effort, but the unique factors that made this possible for the project just completed were totally happenstance based on personalities, and it did not look like the future would allow it to happen again anytime soon. I thought the best thing was to go back to a pure technical role. Trade on any good will I had to get a good assignment in the firmware section. Try and re-capture the fun I had doing the 8051 projects seven years ago.

Rather than become involved in low key petty exchanges with the nominal tech lead, I asked for a transfer to the firmware section. This was my goal eight years earlier, when I first hired in. I found out later that my software section did not want to let me go, but the nominal tech lead had argued strongly that I should go.

Phase IV - Firmware Engineer (2001 .. 2002)

This work was embedded firmware using a 32-bit processor and several custom designed ASICS. The product managed scores of backend SCSI disk drives and presented many virtual disk drive images to many separate host computers. There could be many hundreds of active I/O transactions active at any one time. All of this was asynchronous. The amount of firmware time budgeted to any one individual I/O from a host machine was measured in microseconds.

There were two version of the code: An "instrumented" version with debug hooks that allowed us to find and fix bugs. Then there was the "performance" version with all debug hooks stripped out. This was what we shipped. There was a sort of quantum mechanical effect in that any debug hook introduced or removed would change the sequence of events. Consequently, bugs manifested in different ways in the different versions.

I had official in-company experience with firmware (in the other division), and had lived down the "shades of blue" incident. My new boss promised me that there would be lots of meaty firmware projects, and I would get one. In the mean time I started learning the quirky home-grown operating system, and the debug tools. I learned about the various Fibre Channel protocols. I had excellent help in all of this. There were several good team mates who thought the same way I did. We did not want to play political games, and only thought of the development of the product.

There was a dark side to this, however. I had seen how the firmware section had worked seven-day weeks, and 12-hour days at the end of the previous release cycle. This "death march" went on for six months. I was promised that that was going to be avoided at all costs in the future. Once over in the firmware section, I saw why this sort of work situation developed.

It was a combination of several factors, the biggest of which was the changes in the marketing requests. Again, I heard: "If only we had feature 'X' we could sell so many more." Or an even better one: "Without feature 'X' we do not have a product". As noted earlier, the entire hardware platform was changed in the midst of the project. This exacerbated the second cause of the death march. Entire sections of functionality were given to inexperienced people with little supervision. The resulting code was very complex and brittle. I got so I could make changes to the code without breaking something, but was always worried that I would.

I noticed others had no such worries, and often did break stuff. This OS was fine for a team of eight or so firmware engineers, but it was now used to support the code of twenty or so. Some were aware of the danger, and were careful, others rushed in where others feared to tread. The result was a continual drizzle of bugs and test failures. The number of people who could track down the obscure bugs was few. When major new functionality was merged in, old stuff did not work as well. Even the most careful people could introduce bugs that would not show themselves for months, then take weeks to find and fix.

Marketing came up with other ultimatums: "If it cannot be released by 'Y' date, we do not have a viable product". I looked for the high level manager who would take the R&D lab's side in these arguments, and say things like: "We cannot do this in the timeframe you are talking about." Or, "We should not make this change". "Let's get it out there without this feature, and see what happens". "Let's just get it out, and get a feedback loop started with real users". I do not think accurate information flowed up very high in the management chain. That means it was not wanted. Instead, there was lots of posturing, "Yes sir ! Can do sir" type stuff.

The role of marketing and R&D is the same in a big company as in a small one, only now it is entire departments instead of a few people. Marketing should filter customer requests with experience and some vision of the future. For marketing to say, "if only it had X, we could sell Y more" in the middle of product development is ipso facto a failure of marketing's mission. Marketing should dampen out short term changes in requirements to create a coherent winning strategy.

In an attempt to make these absurd commitments, we got free dinners. Pizza on Saturday. Quality suffered. I was able to hold my own very well in this environment. Most of my peers were in their 20s. They had an enthusiasm for working long hours, and a commitment to the product un-blemished by worries about marketing changes or OS complexity. For many, this environment was all they knew. It reminded me of my old insurance rating job. Except the health insurance premiums were always paid.

I started to feel my age. Free pizza on Saturday did not motivate me like it did some of my teammates. I felt I could not put in too many fewer hours. If I was to be on the team, I had to pull my weight. I did not want to get the reputation of a shirker. It made me tired. All of this overtime work was so un-necessary. "Why, in my day …"

It finally hit me. I had returned to front line firmware work. I was succeeding at it. I could still do it as well or better than I ever could, but... There was no way I could do this till retirement age of 65. It was a combination of energy level and attitude. I did not have the energy for what my attitude saw as un-necessary work. I began to feel a little trapped. I chose this level of work because of my attitude towards becoming a manager. I got what I wanted, but it had changed from what I thought it was going to be. How much of this was age, how much was general big company foolishness, and how much was the specific lab I was in?

While I waited for my "big project", I wrote my own tools based on my old 'C' libraries. Tools to analyze execution path traces. Tools to analyze Fibre channel traces. Even though all existing tools were UNIX based, none of the data was kept in raw text format. People were forever staring at screens of text displayed by the analyzer, but never writing the text into a file where it could be processed by 'grep', or other ad hoc analysis programs. I was able to use my tools to good effect several times.

The biggest re-org of all

The big project never appeared. Instead, there was an acquisition of another company that made similar products. Massive confusion, indecision, and delay. At the end of it all, our product was "deprecated", and no new development was to be done. The other companies' product would go forward.

We were all assured of jobs developing the new product. The word was, we would co-develop with the other product's "architecture". Unfortunately, there were very un-realistic expectations about how this would be done. I listened in growing horror as more and more edicts from on high revealed a total ignorance of how two large very different firmware architectures could be merged. People who knew better avoided eye contact in technical discussions. Posturing was the order of the day.

There was never any doubt in my mind that sooner or later reality would be faced, and all of the current plans would need to drastically change. Such chaos is an opportunity for rapid advancement if the political posturing is done correctly. I never had the slightest urge for slinging BS; all I saw was a year of intense pain and suffering with no technical work of substance to do. Several of my peers did use this chaos, and attained powerful positions in the lab that they kept for the next decade.

Hobbies

I stayed sane by means of recreational programming. I got a loaded PC with lots of memory. I called my projects "etudes", or "studies".

I wrote a "tiler" program that allowed me to generate complex geometric patterns. Besides the good old pentominoes, it would also do the Penrose tiles. A feature allowed me to specify colored line patterns based on these tilings. I generated and saved off some very pretty designs. This program allowed me to explore the "object factory" pattern.

Another effort was a Rubik's cube solver. This was a study in complex object oriented programming. Cube objects, permutation objects, move sequence objects, all inter-related. You could use the mouse to paint the color pattern of a scrambled cube onto the screen. The program would then turn it into a cube object and solve it. You could then ask it for each move one at a time and so solve your cube. It used an algorithm I got from a book, and usually generated a solution of 55 to 65 moves. I had heard speculation that any scrambled cube could be solved in at most 17 moves. I started on a quest to do this. Clever ways to compress permutations so millions of them could be stored in RAM hash tables. Backtracking tree searches by brute force. Assignment of a measure of "scramble" so an optimize algorithm could be used instead of brute force. I would always fail, but each attempt got me closer to the goal. During this time, my program could solve cubes scrambled with 15 moves using my PC. This could be extended to the goal of 17 moves on a supercomputer. It seemed that in a few years, with decreasing RAM prices, increasing CPU speed, and just one more clever insight on my part, I could achieve my goal at home.

I learned Java / Swing at home doing little fun projects. Java finally allowed me to do graphics programming at home on Linux.

Financial

I started out with a salary less than I had at the broker, but ended up making more. The spread in raises between low and high performers was greater than the 3% I saw in 1975. When I became tech lead, I started getting stock options. This was a fatal error on the company's part, as I am cursed to only make a living by hard work. The late 1990's bubble made some of the options worth a lot. They were not yet exercisable, but the total worth was serious money. I had a momentary dream of avarice and un-earned income. Of course, the bubble burst. None of my options were ever worth anything. Sorry about that, but they never should have given me those options.

The top blows off

In the midst of the super re-org, my youngest child turned 21, and I paid his last college tuition payment. There was no conscious change in my attitude, but sub-consciously it was like the top popping off a pressure cooker. The repressed frustrations kept dissolved by the pressure all foamed out.

My career path should take me next to management, but I knew myself too well. I flirted with the thought of part-time work, but there were really no part time jobs to do. In terms of my prior achievements, I had done very little at this company in the entire nine years. Except provide for my family. Now that was done. I handed in my resignation, and left after 'working' out my two weeks' notice.

Interlude (2002 .. 2003)

I was determined to leave the big company behind. I had been doing computer programming for 33 years with only the odd two week vacation during that time. I was tired of programming as a job. Perhaps it was time for a big career change.

I had been thinking about teaching for many years. There is a real need for teachers of mathematics, science, and computer programming at the High School or Junior College level. I thought I could do a good job of this. I was certainly qualified with my degree in Mathematics, and a Masters. The only problem was that teaching did not pay very well.

I had also been working on Needlepoint design for six years or so. I was using my programming hobby to generate original needlepoint designs based on mathematical themes like pentominoes, Penrose tiling, or fractals. I would design, then stitch up needlepoint pictures. Each took a year to design and make. About this time, I had an exhibition at a local needlepoint shop. I also wrote a several page article about my needlepoint designs that were published in the March 2003 issue of *Needlepoint Now* magazine. I thought I could make and sell charts of some of my needlepoint designs. I had good support and advice from the local needlepoint shop. The only problem was that a web based business selling $10 to $20 needlepoint patterns was not likely to pay very well.

My material needs were relatively small, and my wife had a steady part time job that brought in some money. I was in a fey mood. Call it a late midlife crisis.

Teaching

I applied to several local institutions to teach. They were junior college, or vocational school type places. I got two interviews. The interviews went well, and I was asked to "audition" at both places. One wanted someone to teach statistics, the other was computer science. I had to prepare a 15 minute lesson and give it to a group of current faculty and other staff.

Both went badly. I was very nervous, and stumbled in my presentation. My big fear about teaching is getting into an exchange with a student where I cannot think fast enough to hold up my end. In these cases, there were no questions from the "students", but my brain and mouth were not in sync. I got no feedback on why I failed, just a polite "no thanks". I must have been very awful.

Several years later, I think I finally figured out what I had done wrong. I had prepared the lessons based on the way I had been taught in college. I had taken the very abstract mathematics track. I was taught math as a series of formal axioms, theorems, and proofs. Examples were relegated to homework exercises. So, I had prepared a formal explanation of my topic using lots of algebra. At that student level, lessons should be graphic examples.

While preparing my trial lessons, I had also come to realize how much work teaching really is. At the time, I had no idea why I struck out so badly other than my nervousness. I was discouraged, and did not pursue it.

Needlepoint patterns

I sold some patterns at the needlepoint store where I had my exhibition. The owner liked my designs, and gave me lots of advice on what a needlepoint pattern should be. I spent lots of time making about five or six patterns ready to sell. I hired someone to build a web page devoted to my designs. I looked through several trade magazines, and got a mailing list of 100 stores throughout the country that carried these designs.

I did a mass mailing of a brochure, but got zero response. All in all, I spent many, many days and about $300 in trying to sell these patterns. I sold a few based on the web. I think I made a small profit. It worked out to about 5 cents per hour. Several years after I stopped selling the patterns, I would still get requests for one or another of these patterns. Rather than deal with the state sales tax, and income tax issues, I made a copy at Kinko's and just sent it to them for free.

I really enjoyed my mini-retirement. No kids at home, no tuition, a working wife, life was good. I was only slightly worried about the drain on the bank account.

Phase V - Contractor (2003 .. 2004)

This lasted about six months. Then I got a call from an old co-worker at the big company I had just quit. He was in a jam. He now ran a small contracting house (body shop), and needed someone to work on a complex assignment back at the big company. A real good hourly rate. I had real mixed feelings. I acted really reluctant, demanded part time work (a 4 day week), and all of September off. He said "OK". So back to work.

Java again

The project was to build tools to "localize" the entire user interface for a complex line of printers. "Localize" means creating translations for all of the user interface text. A user could select one of 20 languages, and the printer would switch to using that language for all menus, buttons, help messages, etc. It was a complex printer/fax/scanner/copier with a rich GUI interface. The project was to use VMware to run both Linux and Windows on the same laptop. The Linux VM would run the printer simulator, and the Windows VM was to run a custom Java application I was to write. This application would display all strings that needed translation, and allow someone to type in the translation. The app would then communicate the translated strings to the Linux simulator, and you could see just how it would look in the foreign language. The plan was to ship these laptops out to Russia, Poland, Slovenia, Italy, Spain, ... and get the work done cheaply.

The printer simulator was very good. It created an X-window simulation of the printer's display and controls. The simulation was good enough to get the exact pixels right on the GUI interface. This allowed the user to see exactly how a foreign word or phrase would fit in the space available. The only problem was, the simulator ran on the company's UNIX boxes, not on a Wintel Linux box. My first task was to get the simulator to work on the VMware / Linux VM. This was system programming at its best. I made constant progress, and actually got the simulator to boot and display the GUI menus. It would also sort of work, but there were many subtle problems that prevented full functionality. There was a project within the company to get the simulator working on Linux, but it was not a priority. My contracting company ran into political trouble when it asked for help.

The fallback was to have the Java application control real printers, and fly the translators to the plant here to do the work over a week's time. I finished the Java app in time and folks from all over the world were flown in to use it. It worked well, and the project was a success.

During the time I was doing the work, the big company was trying to re-negotiate the terms of the contract to make the cost less. I was being well paid, and the big company wanted to pay 40% less. I would have taken less money, but the body shop did not even ask me. There was a game of brinkmanship, and the week before the first translators were flown in, I was told my contract was canceled, and to stop. The first level manager at the big company who was responsible for the localization pitched a fit, and I was allowed to stay and see the last few weeks of the project through. I was amazed at how heavy handed the big company cost cutting could be. If I had not been there the last two weeks (when the people from around the world were actually using my system), it could have been a disaster. How could the middle management of a fortune 500 company make such a decision?

This project allowed me to learn all about the alphabets of foreign languages, and their UNICODE form within computers. I also learned about XML, and UTF-8. Interesting stuff, with Java being the best way to learn about it. This was a very fun, rewarding project.

Back to where I once belonged

As I was eating lunch in the cafeteria during the last week of the Java contract, another old co-worker came up to me and asked if I wanted to work as a contractor on the project I had left in 2002. He had no idea my current contract was up. This was just pure luck. I said "sure, if it can be part time four days a week". So about a year and a half after I quit the company, I was back working in the same group, working on the same project for about 40% less pay and no benefits.

I tried to work through the body shop I was currently working for, but they refused to take the skimpy 5% margin that was being paid on this greatly reduced salary. I went elsewhere. This was a time when the big company started to flex their muscles, and drastically cut costs. Part of this was massive layoffs and early retirement programs. They also started using contractors (like me) much much more. The pay the contractors got was about 40% less than in years past. The big company succeeded in their cost cutting goals, and places like the body shop I worked for went out of business, or drastically changed the way they did business. I was happy. I was working four days a week, and making much more money that I had selling needlepoint patterns.

I was working with the same people I had left a year ago. The work was finding and fixing bugs in the firmware of the product that the division was selling. I was very effective at this, if a bit slow. Even though I was a contractor, I worked with every one like I was a regular employee. Work was fun, because all I had to do was find and fix programming bugs. I was respected, because I could find and fix tough bugs. I did not need to worry about politics, because I was not an employee.

The project was now working on the very large embedded firmware code base from the company they had acquired a year ago. It was not only large and complex; it was also not modularized very well. Over years of many hands making changes, the code was disorganized and "brittle". Any small change to any part of the code could introduce a bug anywhere else in the code due to unforeseen interactions. My secret to success was I tried to understand all of the code, not just the part I was working on. I also had over 33 years of seeing how computer programs fail. Another famous cliché I admire is: *The definition of an expert in a technical field is a person who has made all possible mistakes in that field.* That was me. A fantastic article that exactly describes this sort of code and programming environment is *Big Ball of Mud*, by Foote. It is both instructive and entertaining to read.

I got to where I enjoyed finding and fixing bugs. It was a lot like detective work. The victim (the running firmware) was usually dead (crashed). It may have been tortured (by tests). There were usually some evidence (various logs from the firmware). I got to do autopsies on the crash dump. Sometimes it took weeks of evidence gathering, and many deaths to find the culprit. Some of these investigations took weeks. Some of these investigations were very challenging, and satisfying to solve.

My most rewarding investigation took three weeks. The failure was not localized to any obvious scenario. There was some evidence to work with, but it never pointed to any specific problem area. I finally realized that the problem was one line missing from a 'C' macro used to for single linked list processing. The OS team (in another site) had converted the linked list code from assembly language to these 'C' macros, and had made a subtle mistake. The slow instrumented builds were correct, only the release performance builds had the bug. I actually had a physical reaction when I found this after looking for it so hard for so long. It was a very difficult problem to solve.

I wrote up the simple one line fix, and asked the OS team to make the change. They responded: NO WAY. Your analysis is incorrect, and there is no bug here. I was amazed. Just take a look at the code. How can you argue? This went up the chain of command, and no one bothered to look at the code. The discussions were all about our team at our site versus the part timer on that team at that other site. Who OWNS this code after all? Totally pre-scientific medieval type reasoning. I was very angry at first, but then just said forget it.

A guy at my site went and made the one line change anyway, and the problem went away. The other site tried to back the change out. A fellow at the other site asked me again for detailed documentation on my fix. I responded that I refused to defend the fix any more, they should just read the code, and remove it if they wanted to. The subject was then dropped, and the fix stayed in.

Phase VI - Full time employee again (2005)

There was a large project going on to create a new product with advanced architecture from a clean sheet of paper. This project had been going on for about a year, and was now staffing up. My old boss from my Java tech lead days was working on it. Many people from his old Java team were assigned to work on this, even though it was embedded firmware. He needed someone with embedded firmware experience to do (informal) technical lead work for him on his portion of the project. He asked me if I would come back as a regular full-time employee. I had left the company on good terms, so this was possible.

I gave this a lot of thought. I was comfortable working part time with no leadership responsibilities. However, I respected my old boss a lot. Besides, the company would re-instate my old rank, pay, seniority, and benefits. A 40% pay hike with full benefits. I accepted. My attitude was totally different from several years ago. I was now in this purely for the money. I was nowhere as frustrated by dumb politics. I had already quit once. Been there, done that. I was not going to quit again because of corporate frustrations. I would be more of a spectator.

Disaster of a project

It took me only a week to realize that the project was a disaster. In every way. There was an academic like stratification of "architects" that were trying to fill a blank sheet of paper without any reference to prototyping, or any other practical consideration. Lots of meetings debating academic-style papers. Lower level employees (like me) asked to leave the room for certain discussions. Lots of C++ religious wars among the elite. Lots of management goals relating to the design documents. NOTHING empirical going on that could be used to measure real progress.

The project started out as a niche offering due to its radically different architecture, but then management started talking about how it would replace the current offering. Huh? No way ! This showed that management was indulging in fantasy, or magic thinking.

Everyone realized the project was doomed. It was a weird work environment, as folks worked hard on re-working abstract documents and endlessly debating and reconsidering old decisions. There was no empirical data to base any of these decisions on. There was a total lack of competence from the upper management team, which did not seem to understand how to actually do a new project from scratch.

I participated by writing my assigned design documents and presenting them to the "architecture" committee. I spent a lot of time in discussions with my local team. They were mostly former Java software programmers. I tried to get them up to speed on what embedded firmware programming entailed. Other teams were actually trying to make prototypes "under the table". Finally, someone who was assigned to model the projected performance of the initial release of the product deduced that it could never meet minimal performance goals as a replacement for the current offering.

BANG !

The entire project was cancelled on one day's notice. All were told that there would be a complete reworking of the division's strategy. Everyone, including those still working on the existing, shipping product, were told they were vulnerable to layoffs, subject to how well their "skill set" fit the new strategy of the division. Just wait two months till management decides the details.

What a long two months. Many folks were very worried about their jobs. The only ones that had anything to do were the people working on the existing product. Management refused to give any hint that even they would be "safe". Finally an announcement was made. Everyone with embedded firmware experience was kept. All managers were kept. All "architects" were kept. The others (most of my team mates) were laid off. I was kept, and assigned back to the same boss I was working for as a part time contractor, doing the same find and fix work on the shipping product. Except for 40% more pay, and full benefits.

Hobbies

During this time my hobby programming revolved around Java and Swing GUI style programming. I got some books on color science and graphic techniques. I wrote programs that allowed me to turn photograph quality pictures into needlepoint patterns. The challenge was to make a 1000x1000 24 bit color picture into a 210x190 9 color picture and make it look good. Another major effort was a program to take a BMP file and make it into a needlepoint chart.

Phase VII - Tapering off (2006 .. 2012)

At this point I was back working on finding and fixing bugs in high performance embedded firmware. My co-workers and immediate managers were all folks I had known for years. I got along well with all of them. There was no real opportunity to do anything really exciting or new. I was as detached as I was able to be.

I just floated along like a corporate drone. This was the first time in my career I did this. The basic reason was my age. I still felt mentally acute. I had no trouble doing the work. Indeed, my experience with past problem solving, and my long study of all areas of this particular codebase made me as effective as anyone else, and more effective than most. I was reaping the benefits of my experience with little effort. Effort was the key as to why I did not try and find a new job. Due to my age (57 to 63), I no longer had the energy to do a clean break, start over, and prove myself again to a new bunch of young strangers. Forget the fact that no one was going to hire someone of my age. Especially in the crappy economy that started in 2008.

Colorado Interlude

A month or so after dust settled from the blown up project, I got the opportunity to move to Colorado Springs and work on a different part of the firmware. It suited company politics and my boss's short term staffing needs. I had long wanted to return to Colorado Springs, where I had lived when I was in the Army. My wife reluctantly agreed to the move, and off I went. She stayed behind and was to move out within six months or so.

I was given the task of installing a third party fibre channel device driver into our firmware. This was a good challenge. My boss was in another state, and I could work as I wanted. I worked on this task most of the time I was in Colorado. I got the work done, and incorporated into the codebase. My wife visited Colorado Springs several times and then changed her mind about the move, and I came back after eight months.

Endian redux

The nature of the work started changing. Management wanted more products using the same firmware codebase. New hardware was designed to make newer products. The theory was that this new hardware would work with our existing firmware, so the effort to have several new products would be small. But when the new hardware was done, it was not quite compatible with the firmware due to word endian (byte ordering) issues.

While looking at the specifications of the new, supposedly compatible hardware, I noticed that the PCI DMA channel had different byte ordering characteristics than the custom ASIC based channel we had been using. It was difficult for me to tell for sure. No one I knew really understood the details. The folks who presumably did understand had said the new hardware was compatible. I did some experiments, isolated the differences, and wrote up a set of papers on the consequences. Major parts of the firmware needed to be changed to be byte ordering agnostic. These changes to the firmware were pervasive, tedious, and hard to test. I thought the architect in charge of the new hardware development should be fired for telling everyone it was compatible with the existing firmware. At first no manager wanted to believe me. I was labeled a trouble maker. The changes needed would turn a simple firmware roll into a massive amount of risky work. We would now have to support several different incompatible hardware platforms with the one codebase.

This would have been tolerable if the firmware was modular, but it was not. We now added a new dimension of complexity (conditional compiles for each hardware platform) to an already convoluted codebase. The testing resources were spread thin. The level of day to day work required to support and test all of this complexity was much more than management assumed it would be.

I was put in charge of a team to investigate the needed firmware changes. I wrote a paper on what byte ordering agnostic code looked like. I wrote a report summarizing what changes were needed in each section of the firmware. The schedule for the new product needed a major slip. The code for the existing product underwent risky changes. Quality slipped. No one was fired.

Changing corporate environment

The work environment changed a lot during my 1994 to 2012 tenure at this company. At first team members were located on the same aisle of cubicles. There were many informal technical discussions. Other communication was by phone. E-mail existed, but was not used to any great extent. As people moved from one team to the next, they were physically moved as well. Often only a few aisles over. Meetings were formal, and all participants were in the same room. There was a lot of proactive work done.

Then cost cutting was used as an excuse to stop physical relocations. Now if you were working on a team, but not co-located, you would be a second-class member. You missed out on many small technical details. Management said it was not a problem because everything was documented. Except it really was a problem.

Next, teams and manager's responsibilities were extended over multiple sites. We were supposed to use conference calls and e-mail to compensate. Except that this did not even come close to the bandwidth needed for a team doing creative technical development. Cross site travel was sometimes used to mitigate this. Unfortunately, there were often edicts from upper management against any travel. Complaints that work could not get done were met with the big lie: "Dispersed teams and cross site technical development works well using the new technologies available".

E-mail took over working life. More and more phone conference meetings grabbed chunks out of the working day. Most people started spending a large chunk of time just reacting to e-mail and meetings. Work life became much more frantic, but less effective. Many people used the new technology to work from home. It starts with reading and answering e-mails at home. Then people were logging in to the corporate systems from home to check on work.

I fought back by using my daily lunch walks to think proactively about work. I walked solo, without any gadgets. I thought about what I should do during the rest of the day. I would also think about work when I was at home, but I never read e-mail or signed on to work from home. I came to greatly resent the increasing pressure to work from home.

Layoffs and Firings

The company started periodic episodes of manpower reductions. This started out with an announced mass layoff. A percent of all employees would be laid off to reduce staff levels. The company had contracted with a third party human resources firm to select who would go. The selections were to be based on race, gender, and age. We were told that this was to make it absolutely "fair". Job performance ranking was specifically excluded from the selection criteria. It seemed to me this was done to make use of the third party firm's legal expertise to make certain no type of legal challenge could be made to any of the selections. When employees talked to their managers about their chances, the managers all answered that they had no input into the process, could not protect anyone, and had no idea of their own chances. It seemed to me that this was an abdication of responsibility by the company, and a breach in the relationship between the company and its employees. In the event, I was not laid off, but some 'A' ranked folks were.

The company then switched to a new policy of constantly firing the lowest ranked employees. There had always been a forced bell curve rank distribution, with 70% mandated 'C' grades, and 3% mandated F grades. Now, the ranking process was being used to routinely fire people. The lower ranked people were "laid off". This was new. Few new people were being hired, so the work load went up and up. Lower ranked people now got zero bonuses in December. It used to be called "profit sharing". Everyone in the company used to get the same percent of their salary as a bonus based on the annual profit of the company as a whole. Now, December bonus was used to reward some people lavishly, and others got nothing.

Cost Cutting and Deadlines

Corporate cost cutting continued. All employees were relocated into much smaller cubicles, often forced to double up with an office mate. Many employees were forced to work from home, and only had access to shared squatter's quarters at the plant. Our lab (containing several hundred systems we used for prototyping and debugging firmware) was now in a separate building and was scheduled to be moved to a different state. This was bad because we often needed to physically connect logic analyzers or fibre channel trace capture equipment to various ports on the devices. All protests were deflected with the excuse that the company global facilities management was yielding lots of savings with these moves, and no one could change any of it.

The closer quarters raised the ambient noise level. One on one discussions now disturbed neighbors. Participation in the constant phone meetings disturbed office mates. Difficulty accessing the lab equipment greatly slowed down the development process. Management's response to these complaints was fiction, fantasy, and the big lie. It was obvious the changes were forced from a very high level, and my boss, boss' boss, and boss' boss' boss had no say in any of this.

Management began to talk about deadlines above all else. "If we do not ship this by XXX date, we will lose $$$$". A memorable comment on a phone conference among middle managers: "If we do not meet this deadline, some of you on this call will lose your jobs". This type of talk had been unprecedented before now. A sort of mass group-think or mass delusion settled over the managers of the lab. Test failures were minimized. Negative comments were unwelcome. I had a bug I was trying to find that was taking a long time. I heard managers say: "Well, it only causes a crash in one of the two redundant processors, the other is OK. The system recovers from the crash OK. This is only a one minute hiccup from the user's perspective. We can ship with this". OK, if you say so.

Consequences

All of this changed the working environment. No one likes to do a crappy job. Now it was not possible to do a good job, because there was too much to do, and not enough time. Everyone at the worker bee level felt this way. I started telling my boss: "I feel I am doing a crappy job. There is too much to do, so I am not doing a good job on some of this". My boss said: "I know, but what can we do ? Just do as best as you can." I always had an 'A' ranking, and got substantial bonuses. But I was still appalled at the changes.

We released a crappy product, but had deluded ourselves it was "OK". We went immediately into a new release cycle to put out a "bug fix release". But, we were also supposed to be working on future products as well. No relief from having too much work to do, to do any of it well.

This work environment was a descent from feudalism. Now we had more of a bureaucratic, totalitarian state like the old USSR. Bosses at all levels were just bureaucrats in constant fear of their own superiors. There were purges at high levels to stoke this fear. At the worker-bee level we were now just micromanaged serfs. We were overworked, and clearly expendable. Some sucked up to the system. Some kept their heads down in constant fear of denunciation.

Fun New Project

During this time, I was given a new project to develop a major component for a next generation project the lab was starting to work on. This involved managing 300 asynchronous devices during recovery from glitches or topology changes on SATA links. No one in the lab had any experience with this new technology, so I was in the fun position of learning as I went along. This was the way I had worked earlier in my career, so I was happy with this assignment.

This work progressed well. I prototyped and explored, and got the initial version of firmware to work with this technology. I started a cycle of refinement and testing to create a final shipping quality component. This also went as well as possible given the equipment on hand. Due to cost constraints, we did not have the hardware in the lab to test for the full 300 device configurations.

At this point our team got a new boss. My boss for the last four years was assigned a new team, and our team picked up a new boss. I knew him from when he was a peer developer. The new boss had a much different approach to management. He was by the book. He held an initial meeting where he told us how we would now be working: The concept of prototype, and functionality refinement was not in his world view. His perspective was to document a design, then implement it, and then test it. Even if no one had experience with the relevant technology. I was as open and straightforward as I could be about my work progress, but it was as if he spoke a different language. I was disappointed, but I had worked with all types of bosses and figured it would work out OK.

Shit hits the fan

After half a year, the failures of the older product in the field began to mount up. Upper management came down hard on our lab. The lab manager was fired. Other middle managers were re-assigned. A new guy was brought in as department boss, and his message was: "You guys are screw ups. That crappy product was your fault. You must be punished. Remedial action is necessary". This made me (and others) angry. We knew how to make a quality product. We had done it for years. We were prevented from doing it in this case by management insistence on staffing levels vs. the number and timing of new products in the development pipeline. We were releasing them before they were ready. The manager who was fired was a scape goat. We all knew that. Management was the problem, not us worker bees.

There was remedial action. Many meetings started up. All the low level managers started micro-managing to a very detailed schedule. Gone were the days of playing detective on bugs, or prototyping and exploring the new technology needed for the new product. That stuff could not be quantified in a schedule. (At least not in the schedule as this management team set it up). Any changes in the schedule or any variance in the schedule became topic for long tedious middle management meetings. Work priorities changed day to day as the new managers tried to decide how much to work on fixing the old product, or how much to work on the future product. A tremendous climate of fear descended on the lab. We already had one head on a spike (our former lab manager) to instill the fear.

My relationship with work had changed in a major way. I was no longer happy to explore new technology, or learn new techniques. I was unhappy that the current work environment now made it almost impossible to work effectively. I started to wonder: Is this just old age? Was I becoming a curmudgeon? Or was this the first time in my 40-year career that the working environment was so dysfunctional?

Ranking Changes

Unrelated to our lab's remedial actions, the corporation changed ranking in a major way. Management said 30% of us must be ranked as "D", with no bonus. This was on top of the already mandated 5% "F" ranking. Were so many really "D" quality workers? An immediate question back to management was: "OK, what do I need to do different to raise to a "C" level"? There was no real answer, because the "D" ranking was not really a measure of performance. This also made everyone angry. One guy on my team immediately quit. One of the bosses quit rather than carry out these rankings. It seems immoral to me to use an individual's ranking as punishment for something beyond their control. The obvious reaction is: If my career is jeopardized by a crappy ranking that is really due to some dysfunctional management goal of the organization I am in, then obviously it is time for a new organization.

I never understood the real reason for hijacking the ranking system for a non-ranking purpose. After all, if you need to get rid of people, you can just say that, and get rid of them regardless of their ranking. It had been done before. It turns out that many other large corporations implemented similar changes to their ranking at the same time. Some corporate zeitgeist. In any case, the attitude of the corporation's employees towards the corporation changed for the worse. This was exacerbated by the great recession underway in the world economy. Lots of unhappiness to go around.

At my next ranking, my boss showed me my peer feedback, many of which said "One of the best engineers in the lab". He then dropped my ranking from "A" to "C". I was stunned. I asked him if he really thought I was only an average member of the team, or was this ranking due to the political pressures. His response was "You are just an average member of the team." I knew what I had done on the new technology development, and I knew what my team members' abilities were because they were always in my cube asking for consultations and advice. Either I was a sad case of delusional senility, my boss was clueless, or my boss was dishonest.

Test (2010 .. 2012)

I decided I needed to make a change to something technically different, to take my mind off my current working environment. I asked for a transfer to the test organization. The test group did C++ programming to create many elaborate automated tests. That would be a change. Besides, the manager of the test group was my former manager from two years ago, and he thought I was a good worker. Persuading my current boss to let me go was not hard; after all, I was only a "C" worker to him.

I had worked closely with many of the test team members. The codebase used by the test team was well written C++ that had evolved over several years, and was a joy to work with. The test team was 95% located at our site, and all interactions were face to face. On the test team I was still writing code and solving problems. They were just different problems, and that helped keep my mind off the larger organizational follies.

I was very effective in test because of my experience in the firmware. I knew where all the bodies were buried. I worked in test for several years, and came to enjoy my job again.

Fiasco (2011)

Development on the new product continued. About two months prior to release, a member of my old team told me he was re-writing the code I had written for it. He said there were some bugs found on large configurations. He looked at my code, and thought it was not maintainable. He was going to re-write it in a structured fashion. I argued with him a little, but he was determined to re-write it. I thought the code was inherently complex due to the functionality it supported. I thought my code could be easily changed to fix the newly found bugs. I thought this old teammate did not want to do the work (or was unable to do the work) it would take to understand my code. It was his call, I was working in test, and not involved.

Later on, I heard that my old team was asking for a month's delay in releasing the new product so the re-write could be completed. I thought how naive can you be? I went to my boss in the test organization, and asked for protection. I would give all consulting advice needed, but did NOT want to be drafted back to the old team. It had been a year since I had left, my code never had any issues in that time, and my old team had judged me as a mediocre performer. I went to my boss's boss and said the same thing. They both thought I was being paranoid because at that point no one was even asking for me, and it was not my business. No one wanted my old code. They were going to re-write it instead. But I knew the new department manager was not an idiot. He was not so stupid as to delay product release for a re-write of a complex part of the code at that late date.

Huge panic. The department manager flew in from California; the lab manager flew in from Colorado, and took a hotel room for the duration. Lots of high level meetings to assess the situation. I was interviewed by the head architect and told him I was happy to consult and give advice, but I did not want to work with the old team again.

Finally, there was a big meeting with the department manager and all bosses to decide what to do about the requested delay. I was asked to attend. I sat with the other testers against the outer wall. Lots of fear in the room. My old team mate criticized my code as complex and un-maintainable. I was asked about my code. I said all criticisms of it were valid: it was indeed a prototype morphed into production code, and it was necessarily complex, as it needed to manage over 300 asynchronous devices with all of their error modes. Test failures, the new code, and schedule were discussed in depth. I was silent. Finally, the department boss asked someone at the table to move over and pointed to me. "Please sit at the table". I was told I was a member of my old team again, release would not be delayed, and everyone would work 24/7 from now till release to ensure my old code would pass the failing tests. Mandated progress meetings 7 days a week at 9:00 AM. After the meeting I told the department head I was too old, and would only be able to work 6 days a week. He said "OK".

This was the absolute worst outcome for me. My entire career was based on planning the work so I could maintain an even strain. Now I was to work Saturdays in order to save my ex-boss's ass, to save the corporation that was now crapping all over the low-level employees.

I participated 6 days a week. Worked Easter day. Made a few changes to my old code. All tests passed. The product was released, and over the next year there were no issues in the field due to my code. As far as I could tell there were no negative consequences to my old team or old boss for being so stupid as to think they could re-write a major complex part of the firmware a few months prior to release.

Final Task

After the product shipped, I went back to my old position on the test team. The major task during my last year there was to document testing procedures and record a video walk-through of my firmware code in preparation for transferring ownership of the product to a team in India. A group of very competent and nice people from India came over to our lab and spent a month reviewing these documents and training on the product we had just released.

Hobby

As the work environment got worse and worse, my hobby programming got better and better. I got a quad core 4GB Dell PC and set it up to run Linux. I decided to go after high performance large data type programs.

I did not want to learn X-windows programming, so I created a simple

Java application to take bitmap images from the disk and display them. The display program was controlled by messages passed in a Linux pipe. The images were created on disk by the application programs. All application programming was done in Linux C++. I set up a multi-processing harness so I could use all four of the CPU cores on the same problem. I translated most of my graphics library from Java to C++.

One of the first projects I did was to revive the Rubik's Cube solver. I was able to fit seven moves into a 1 GB hash table, and do a ten move deep backtracking algorithm that used all four cores. It took two days (48 hours) to look for seventeen move solutions to the Rubik's Cube. I ran many trials where I scrambled the cube hundreds of moves. I input the scrambled configuration into the program, and started it up. In all cases it found a solution. It is fun to look at how the solution works. Standard solution methods described in books, and used by people consist of many, many moves. You look at certain aspects of the cube, and perform simple three or four move sequences to slowly build up the final solution. If you watch these methods work, you see the solution slowly build up layer by layer. With my new method, it takes only 17 moves, and it looks like nothing is happening for 13 or so of those moves. It looks like random changes, and then the final moves put the entire cube back into order. That is awesome to watch. This was the culmination of a project I had been working on (off and on) for 15 years.

Other projects included an improved Fractal imager, and an improved Penrose tiles drawer. These new versions take advantage of 4GB memory and multiple CPU cores for fast processing.

Retirement (2012)

A year after the fiasco, the company announced an early retirement program where folks would get two years of subsidized health insurance, and a year's salary paid into an IRA. The company wanted to lay off a large number of people, and wanted to start by getting rid of old farts like me. I qualified for the offer. I had been making the maximum contribution to my 401-k since I was re-hired in 2005, and had accumulated sufficient savings. I was eligible for social security. After the two years' subsidized health insurance ran out I would be eligible for Medicare. I took the offer and retired at the end of August 2012. The week prior to my retirement, the department head during the fiasco came to my cubicle and said "Thank You" for my participation in the release of the last product.

Projects

Although I was unemployed and not getting paid, I continued to work the same schedule as before on my own projects at home. I worked on a few large new projects, and continued my hobbies.

The web page I had commissioned during my needlepoint chart sales days had long been abandoned. Meanwhile I had new needlepoint canvases as well as many large images of Penrose and pentomino tilings that would be worth displaying on the web. I decided to learn how to make and manage a web page. I got books on HTML and Java Script, and set to work. I was happy with the results, but because I wrote and typed in all of the HTML myself it was tedious to create and maintain.

My son had been drawing a graphic diary of his life in Japan for several years. He was posting the images to a blog site, but wanted to publish each year's worth in a paperback book. He had used a buddy of his in Japan to do the first year. I volunteered to do the next volume. To do this I bought Adobe InDesign and set to work learning what it takes to produce a print ready PDF file for a paperback book. I published several different volumes in the series and shipped them to Japan, where he sold them at conventions in Tokyo. This was a large but rewarding project, and I enjoyed working closely with my son.

My son was disappointed in how his stuff was presented on the blog site he was using. I volunteered to build him a web site to his specification. He wanted fancy indexing and language switching options. He also wanted automatic daily postings of each day's panel. I decided to use PHP for the server side work. Much of this job was converting and re-formatting his original art into smaller GIF images suitable for web display. Needless to say, I wrote many programs to make all of this automatic. This project became almost like a real job. My son was very picky about the visual presentation and operation of the site. Again, I enjoyed working with him.

Hobby

I abandoned LINUX and switched to MS Windows for my hobby horses. I wanted to make interactive GUI programs. I had written these types of programs in my first year in the fortune 500 company, but a lot had changed since then. My first interactive project was a Sudoku solver.

After that I made a fancier image renderer and wrote programs that mapped photographs of stone and tile surfaces onto my Pentomino and Penrose tilings.

I fooled around with making thousands of images and turning them into MP4 videos. I did several different types, but the largest category was of zooming into a fractal image to reveal more and more details.

As I write this I continue to ride my hobby horses, but at a reduced gait.

Acknowledgement

My wife Teri read the manuscript several times and her suggested edits made it much better.

Thanks, Teri.

Made in the USA
Monee, IL
04 November 2026

67377494R00066